Baby's Names

Baby's Names

JENNY SAVILLE

WARD LOCK

A WARD LOCK BOOK

First published in the UK in 1994 by Ward Lock
Villiers House, 41/47 Strand, London WC2N 5JE

A Cassell Imprint

Reprinted 1994

Copyright © Jenny Saville 1994

Previously published in 1987 and reprinted in 1989, 1990 (twice), 1991 and 1992

Distributed in the United States
by Sterling Publishing Co., Inc.
387 Park Avenue South, New York, NY 10016–8810

Distributed in Australia
by Capricorn Link (Australia) Pty Ltd
2/13 Carrington Road, Castle Hill, NSW 2154

British Library Cataloguing-in-Publication Data
A catalogue record for this book is available from the British library

ISBN 0–7063–7292–1

Typeset by Columns of Reading

Printed and bound in Great Britain by
Biddles Ltd, Guildford and King's Lynn

Introduction

There can be few things more likely to cause arguments than the naming of a baby – it's something all parents-to-be are expected to have decided upon long before the birth, and it's something on which everyone you know has an opinion. Perhaps this is because names really are fascinating. Why, for example, do names come into fashion or become unpopular? Sometimes fashions in names have been influenced by historical events, such as the Norman Conquest, which ousted many Saxon names. Trends have been set by the Church. After the Reformation, for example, Protestant parents tended to use names from the Bible, particularly the Old Testament, rather than giving their children saints' names. The Puritans favoured the abstract 'virtue' names, such as Felicity, Grace and Joy. Some names have been invented by authors, perhaps the best-known example being Wendy, invented by J.M. Barrie for his *Peter Pan*. Names have been popularized by famous people from royalty to rock stars. Hollywood has started many new trends, with children being named not only after the actors and actresses but also after the fictional characters they portrayed in popular films. Television has also been influential.

What should you take into consideration when choosing a name, particularly when you are being bombarded with suggestions from your friends, neighbours and well-meaning relations, or when names come leaping out at you from the pages of all the books you read or from television programmes you watch? First of all, it is a good idea to consider the sound of the first name or names when used with the child's surname, making sure at the same time you avoid such combinations as Roland Hamm, Warren Pease and Issy Awlright. Look also at the child's planned initials. Do they spell a word, and, if so, is it one you think your child would be happy to live with? You'll have to be especially careful when naming a daughter as her initials may change on marriage. It might be wiser to avoid using names starting with a vowel for a girl's middle name or names, so that P.I.N. does not become P.I.G. one day, for example.

Do you think it is important to choose a name which indicates the child's sex, or would you prefer a name which is neither strongly masculine nor feminine, such as Hilary, Carol, Esme or Stacey?

Perhaps you would like to name your child after a famous person, or after a character from literature. Or, maybe you feel names should have some religious significance. This book contains many examples of well-known people and of names associated with books, songs and films which will help you make your choice. People associated with a particular name can often sway parents in its favour, or just as easily turn them against the name.

In some families it is traditional to name children after relatives, a grandparent, for example. If you are naming your child after a relation you might wish to avoid duplication within your close family circle, both of names and possibly even of initials – otherwise you may find that when your son grows up he will be opening all his father's mail, and vice versa.

Is the original meaning of a name important to you? Check it in this book to make sure you like the meaning of the name you are considering and to make sure it is not wildly inappropriate. Consider looking up the word in a dictionary (and even in a slang dictionary) to make certain it has no untoward associations.

Do you like the diminutives of the name you have decided upon or will you regret your choice when your daughter Margaret becomes Maggie or when you find that your son Edward is called Ted by all his friends?

Will the pronunciation or spelling of the name cause difficulty? If you're in doubt try it out on friends. Less common names might present more of a problem here, although many very popular traditional names have alternative spellings.

Is the name you have in mind a fashionable one – and if so is it likely to 'date' your child? Naming a baby after a currently popular record, film or television personality may allow people to pinpoint its approximate date of birth in years to come. Despite this, prevailing fashion and popular culture probably influence parents more than anything else when deciding on a name for their baby. Many parents try to find a name which is neither too popular within their social circle nor completely unfashionable.

Do you want a traditional name or would you prefer something unusual, perhaps to assert your child's individuality? Through the ages some parents have invented names, by combining the mother's and the father's name, for example. Others turn to less usual names from the past – it has always been the practice to revive the names of almost forgotten heroes from fact or legend.

7

Would you like your child's name to reflect its national or regional heritage? If you have a Russian ancestor, for example, you may decide on Tamara for your baby daughter. Irish, Scottish and Welsh parents have a wealth of names to choose from.

Finally, think of your child before yourself. Will he or she feel happy with and be proud of the name you have chosen? Your daughter may not thank you for naming her Doncaster because you had a good day at the races on the day she was born! Don't pick a name to reflect your own hopes or beliefs but rather what you hope for your child.

In this book (b) indicates a boy's name and (g) a girl's name.

Aaron (b) Possibly Egyptian or Hebrew; biblical, meaning obscure. In the Bible, this name was given to Moses's brother.

Aaron Copland, the American composer, is perhaps best known for his orchestral suites: *Billy the Kid* (1938), *A Lincoln Portrait* (1942) and *Appalachian Spring* (1944).

Abigail (g) Hebrew; biblical; 'father's joy', 'father rejoiced'. In the Bible, Abigail was one of the wives of King David and a well-known heroine of the scriptures. It was a popular middle-class name in Britain in the seventeenth century, but may have fallen from favour somewhat when it was used by Beaumont and Fletcher in their play, *The Scornful Ladie*, when it was used for a lady's maid, confidante of the heroine.

Abraham (b) Hebrew; biblical; 'father of a multitude'. In the Bible Abraham was father of the Hebrew people, who came from the Chaldean town of Ur to Canaan (*Genesis*

11–25). In Britain the name Abraham was used from the time of the Reformation, when Old Testament names became popular. Many Abrahams have been named after the sixteenth President of the United States of America, Abraham Lincoln (1809–65). He led the north in the American Civil War, proclaiming that on and after 1st January 1863, all slaves in states or parts of states in rebellion should be freed. He was assassinated on 14th April 1865 at a Washington theatre by an actor, J. Wilkes Booth, and he died early the next day.

An 'Abraham Newland' was nineteenth-century slang for a bank note because the signature of Newland, the cashier of the Bank of England, appeared on bank notes in the early 1800s.

Adam (b) Hebrew; biblical from *adamah*, 'red skin' or 'earth'. In the Bible Adam is the first man created by God (*Genesis* 2). The name became well known in the north of England in the Middle Ages, because of an outlaw and celebrated archer, Adam Bell, a Robin-Hood figure. Shakespeare uses the name for a faithful old servant in the comedy *As You Like It*.

Famous Adams include Adam Smith (1723–90), the Scottish economist and philosopher, author of *Inquiry into the Nature and Causes of the Wealth of Nations*. Modern-day children given the name Adam may be named after the singer and actor, Adam Faith.

Adelaide (g) Teutonic; 'noble kind', 'noble sort'. The name was popularized by Queen Adelaide (1792–1849), born Princess Adelaide of Saxe-Coburg and Meiningen. In 1818 she married the then Duke of Clarence, who later became William IV.

10

Adrian (b) Latin, 'of the Adriatic'. Adrian IV, Nicolas Breakspear, was the only Englishman to become pope (1154–59).

Adrienne (g) French feminine form of Adrian.

Agatha (g) Greek; 'good'. St Agatha of Sicily (third century) was a beautiful Christian girl, tortured by Quintianus, governor of Sicily. Her veil is said to have saved the city of Catania from a stream of molten lava which poured down from Mount Etna some twelve months after her death. The local people were said to have taken her veil from her tomb and carried it towards the lava, which then miraculously changed course. St Agatha is the patron saint of bell-founders and her name is called upon for protection from fire. Introduced into Britain by the Normans, the name again became popular from the nineteenth century, but has been very little used in recent years. A famous Agatha was the celebrated author of detective novels, Agatha Christie.

Agnes (g) from the Greek 'pure, chaste' rather than the Latin 'lamb'. St Agnes (third-century Christian martyr), was only 12 or 13 years old when she is said to have consecrated her life to Christ and refused to marry the son of the prefect of Rome, despite attempts by the prefect to shame her and torture her. The name was very popular from the twelfth to sixteenth centuries and was revived during the nineteenth century, but nowadays it has again fallen out of fashion.

Aidan (b) Gaelic; 'fire, fiery one'. St Aidan was an Irish missionary (c. 600-651) who founded the monastery of Lindisfarne in Northumbria.

Aisha, Ayesha (g) From the favourite wife of the prophet Mohammed.

Alan, Allan, Allen, Alun (b) Celtic, origin unknown but

11

possibly meaning 'peace'. The name was introduced to Britain by the Normans. Alan Ladd (1913–1964) the American tough-guy film star is amongst those with this name.

Alastair, Alistair, Allister (b) Gaelic form of Alexander.

Alban (b) Latin; 'of Alba', 'white'. St Alban, third century, was the first British martyr stoned to death at Verulamium, later called St Albans after him. His feast day is 22nd June. The name Alban was favoured by the nineteenth-century Tractarians.

Albert (b) Old German; 'nobly bright'. Albert was first introduced to Britain by the Normans though it was very little used until it was reintroduced by the future Prince Consort of England who married Queen Victoria in February 1840. His encouragement of the arts was highlighted in the Great Exhibition of 1851 and his interests included education, science, social and industrial reform.

Alberta (g) Feminine form of Albert, which became popular in the nineteenth century in honour of the Prince Consort. Variants include **Albertine** and **Albertha**.

Aldous (b) Old German, 'old'. The name has been used in England since the thirteenth century. A well-known person who bore the name was Aldous Huxley (1894–1963) the English essayist and novelist, whose works include *Crome Yellow*, *Antic Hay* and *Brave New World*. Variants of the name include **Aldus**, **Elden** and **Elton**.

Alexander (b) Greek; 'defender, protector of men'. A name popular for thousands of years. The most famous Alexander is without doubt the Macedonian king, Alexander the Great (356–322 BC). Alexander was appointed regent during his father's absence at war, when he was only 16 years old. He became king before he was twenty and had soon conquered Persia, most of the cities of Asia Minor, Syria, Egypt (where he founded Alexandria) and Babylon. He was also responsible for spreading the Greek language and culture throughout his empire.

Other celebrated Alexanders include eight popes; three Russian emperors and three kings of Scotland. Sir Alexander Korda (Sandor Corda), (1893–1956) is the Hungarian director and producer who settled in Britain in 1930 and revitalized the British film industry. The story of another Alexander — Alexander Nevsky, the thirteenth-century Russian prince and military hero — is told in Sergei Eistenstein's epic film.

Alexandra, Alexandrina, Alix (g) Feminine form of Alexander. The name has been in use since the first century but owes its popularity mainly to Queen Alexandra (1844–1925), the eldest daughter of the Danish king, Christian IX, who married the eldest son of Queen Victoria, the future Edward VII in 1863. A much-loved queen, she founded the Queen Alexandra's Royal Army Nursing Corps.

Alexei, Alexis (b), **Alexia** (g) Russian versions of Alexander.

Alfred (b) Teutonic; 'elf-counsel'. Made famous by Alfred, the king of the West Saxons (849–99), the only English king to be called 'Great'. Alfred not only managed to repel the Danish invaders and helped to consolidate England into one united monarchy but he reformed existing laws and made new laws of his own. He also encouraged learning by setting up schools.

13

The name Alfred lost popularity between the 16th and 18th centuries, but re-emerged again in the 19th century. Other famous Alfreds include poets, Alfred de Musset (1810–1857), and Alfred, 1st Baron Tennyson (1809–92) and the Swedish inventor Alfred Nobel (1833–96) who left most of his money to found the annual prizes which bear his name. The 1966 film *Alfie* starred Michael Caine as a carefree Cockney bachelor intent on a series of amorous conquests. It was an enormous box-office success.

Alice (g) Old German 'nobility'. Alice was introduced to Britain by the Normans and has many variants such as **Alison, Alissa, Alicia, Alyson, Alicen, Alycia**. Alice was amongst the top twenty girls' names in 1700, 1800 and 1900 and is still the choice of many parents nowadays. One of Queen Victoria's daughters was called Alice, and, of course, the publication of Lewis Carroll's *Alice's Adventures in Wonderland* helped to make the name a firm favourite. The American film star of the thirties and forties, Alice Faye, may also have been responsible for keeping the name in people's minds.

Alma (g) This name became popular after the Crimean Battle of Alma in 1854. Not only babies, but many streets in Britain were named after this victory.

Alwyn, Aylwyn, Alvin (b), **Alvina** (g) Teutonic; 'noble friend'.

Amanda (g) Latin; 'fit to be loved'. Popular Restoration name used by Sir John Vanburgh in his first comedy *The Relapse* (1696). A very popular name in the twentieth century. Variants include **Mandi, Mandy**.

Amber (g) From the yellow fossil resin.

Amelia (g) possibly Old German; 'busy'. Used by

Shakespeare in *The Comedy of Errors*. Amelia Earhart (1898–1937) was the first woman to fly the Atlantic (1928). Her plane was lost over the Pacific in 1937.

Amity (g) One of the 'virtue' names.

Amy (g) French; 'loved'. The name was in vogue during the seventeenth century and again fashionable in the nineteenth and twentieth centuries. Another airwoman, Amy Johnson (1903–41), may have added to the name's more recent appeal. Variants include **Aimée**.

Andrea (g) Italian, feminine form of Andrew. Variants include **Aindrea**.

Andrew, André (b) Greek; 'manly'. Always an outstanding favourite. St Andrew the Apostle, one of the first disciples of Christ, is the patron saint of Scotland. His feast day is 30th November. The name Andrew was used in old plays for a man-servant. In Shakespeare's *Twelfth Night* Andrew Aguecheek is the duped and much-maligned steward.

Aneurin (b) Welsh; 'true gold'. The British Labour politician, Aneurin Bevan (1897–1960), was the spokesman for the Welsh miners in the 1926 General Strike. He was appointed minister of Health in the 1945 Labour government and introduced the National Health Service in 1948.

Angel (b), **Angela, Angelica, Angelina, Angie** (g) Greek; 'angelic one', 'messenger'. Angel was Tess's husband in Thomas Hardy's book, *Tess of the D'Urbevilles*. Angelica Kauffmann (1741–1807), the Swiss decorative painter, lived in London from 1766 to 1781 during which time she was nominated one of the first Royal Academicians. The British actress and musical star, Angela Lansbury, appeared in a host of films including *The Dark at the Top of the Stairs*.

15

Angus (b) Celtic; 'one choice'. A common Scottish name, used from the third century BC.

Ann, Anna, Anne (g) from the Hebrew, Hannah. Anna, the Greek form, was the name chosen by the author Tolstoy for the heroine of his second great work, *Anna Karenina* (1874–76). Anna Mary Moses (1860–1961), better known as Grandma Moses, was a popular American primitive artist who began to paint — mainly scenes from her youth — at the age of 75. Anna Sewell (1820–78) was the author of the popular book, *Black Beauty* (1877), perhaps the most celebrated novel about horses.

St Anne, by tradition the mother of the Virgin Mary, is the patron saint of carpenters. Her feast day is 26th July. She is depicted in many Renaissance works of art, particularly in scenes of the life of the Virgin and in pictures of the Holy Family. Ann/Anne has been a favourite name in Britain since the seventeenth century. Queen Anne (1665–1714), the last Stuart sovereign, helped to popularise the name, though she is only one of many royal Annes who include, Anne Boleyn, Anne of Cleves, Anne of Bohemia, Anne of Brittany, Anne of Denmark and, most recently, Princess Anne, born in 1950, the daughter of Queen Elizabeth II. The name has many compounds, derivatives and diminutives, including **Anita, Annette, Anais, Annie, Anika, Nan, Nanette, Nancy, Annemarie, Annalisa, Annabel, Annabella.**

Anselm (b) Old German; 'helmet of God'.

Anthea (g) Greek, poetic, 'flowery', 'lady, maiden, of flowers'.

Anthony, Antony (b), **Antonia, Antoinette** (g) Latin; 'inestimable' or Greek; 'flourishing'. Anthony was originally popularized by several Roman emperors including the benevolent Antonius Pius (86–161), during whose happy and peaceful reign the Antonine Wall was built in Scotland to define the northern boundary of the Roman Empire. Many saints helped to make the name a favourite, particularly the hermit saint Anthony the Great (251–356), regarded as the father of Christian monasticism, who is said to have lived to the age of 105; and St Anthony of Padua (1195–1231), who joined the order of St Augustine but in 1220 joined the Franciscans, becoming a close friend of St Francis. He is said to have been a great speaker and St Francis entrusted to him much of the order's educational work. Several legends are told about this saint, including the story of the ass which knelt before the sacrament, in order to convert a man in Toulouse. St Anthony of Padua is said to have preached to the fishes when men would not listen to him and he is therefore the patron of the lower animals. He is also the patron saint of Padua and of lost property!

April, Avril (g) Latin. The name is derived from the name of the calendar month.

Arabella, Arabelle (g) Scottish, from the Latin; 'yielding to prayer'. In use since the thirteenth century. Diminutives include **Bella**.

Arlene, Aline, Alena, Alina, Alene (g) Old German; 'nobility'.

Arthur (b) Perhaps from the Anglo-Saxon; 'valorous'. Made known by the half-legendary king of the 6th century, who appears in British, Breton, Cornish, Welsh, Scottish and Cumbrian legend. According to literature he was born at Tintagel, a castle in Cornwall, and died at Glastonbury.

17

Prince Arthur (1187–1203) was the heir to the English throne but was imprisoned by the future king John, and murdered on his orders in France. Another Prince Arthur (1486–1502) was the eldest son of Henry VII.

The name Arthur returned to favour in the nineteenth century, helped by the Victorian taste for things medieval and by the popularity of Arthur Wellesley, first Duke of Wellington (1769–1852). He was the victor of many battles including Waterloo, for which he was rewarded with the Hampshire estate of Stratfield Saye. Queen Victoria's third son, and seventh child, was born on the Duke of Wellington's eighty-first birthday and was christened Arthur after the Duke, who became his godfather.

Asa (b) Hebrew; 'healer'. A biblical name.

Asher (b) Hebrew; 'happy'.

Ashley (b) and (g) Old English; 'ash tree clearing'.

Astra (g) Greek; 'like a star'.

Astrid (g) Old German; 'divine strength'.

Aubrey (b) Old German; 'fairy king'. Variations include **Oberon**, the king of the fairies and used as a character by Shakespeare in his play, *Midsummer Night's Dream*, and **Alberic** the German king of the Elves, who features in Wagner's operatic cycle *The Ring of the Nibelung*. Aubrey Beardsley (1872–98), the artist is known for his black-and-white, *art nouveau* book illustrations.

Audrey (g) Anglo-Saxon, 'noble might', a contraction of Etheldreda, the foundress of Ely Cathedral in

Cambridgeshire. At the annual fair of St Audrey, held in the isle of Ely, cheap, showy lace and ornaments were sold and this is the origin of the word tawdry for something gaudy, in poor taste. In Shakespeare's *As You Like It* Audrey is a country wench who jilts William for Touchstone.

Augusta, Augustina (g), **Augustin, Augustus, Augie, Austin** (b) Latin; 'majestic'. Augustus was the title of Roman emperors. St Augustin (5th century) was one of the four Fathers of the Church, who became Bishop of Hippo in Africa. Another St Augustine (died 604) was the first Archbishop of Canterbury. Augustus was the name given to three electors of Saxony, two of whom were in addition kings of Poland.

Aurora, Aurore (g) Latin; 'dawn'.

Barbara (g) Latin; 'foreign, stranger'. Third-century patron saint of artillery, soldiers, gunsmiths and fire fighters. She is invoked to protect against accidents and sudden death. According to legend her father imprisoned her in a high tower, afraid she would marry and leave him, and, when he found she had secretly become a Christian, he had her tortured and killed. The cult of the saint and the name Barbara were very popular in pre-Reformation times. The name returned to favour in the twentieth century.

Barnabas, Barnaby, Barney (b) Aramaic; 'son of exhortation'. St Barnabas, whose feast day is 11th June, was a disciple of St Paul and also a missionary. The name was used by Charles Dickens for the simple lad in his novel *Barnaby Rudge*.

Barry (b) Celtic; 'looking straight at the mark, good marksman'. This was a name used particularly in Ireland. W. M. Thackeray's novel *Barry Lyndon*, the tale of an 18th-century Irish gentleman of fortune, became a 1975 film produced by director Stanley Kubrick.

Bartholomew (b) Probably Hebrew; 'son of the furrows'. One of Christ's disciples about whom little is known. His saint's day is 24th August and, on this day, the Bartholomew Fair was held annually between 1133–1855, at West Smithfield in London, to raise money for St Bartholomew's Hospital.

Basil (b) Greek; 'king-like'.

Beatrice, Beatrix (g) Latin; 'giver of joy'. Beatrice was the heroine of Dante's *La Divina Commedia* (*c.* 1300), and this helped make the name popular. The name was revived by the nineteenth-century Pre-Raphaelite Brotherhood. The English author Beatrix Potter (1866–1943) is well known for her children's books. Recently popularized by Princess Beatrice. Modern variants of the name include **Trixie**, and pet forms include **Bea, Beattie**.

Beau (b) French; 'handsome'.

Belinda (g) Latin and Norse; 'serpent-like'. Used from the eighteenth century in Britain. Belinda was the heroine of Alexander Pope's serio-comical poem *The Rape of the Lock*, apparently based on a real incident.

Benedict (b) Latin; 'blessed'. A popular Pre-Reformation name, St Benedict was born near Spoleto in Italy and became the sixth-century founder of the Benedictine order. At the great monastery he established at Monte Cassino he wrote the basic rules which have served as an outline for most of Western monasticism. Among other saints with this name was St Benedict Biscop (*c.* 628–689), abbot of St

21

Peter's, Canterbury and founder of monasteries in Wearmouth and at Jarrow. Fifteen popes also bore the name Benedict, two of whom assumed the title Benedict XIII. Pope Benedict XIV (Prospero Lambertini, 1675–1758) founded chairs of Physics, Mathematics and Chemistry in Rome and did much to encourage the learning of literature and science. In his comedy *Much Ado About Nothing* Shakespeare's character, Benedick, is a sworn bachelor who finally marries Beatrice. Variants and diminutives of this name include **Ben, Benet, Bennet, Bennie, Benny**.

Benjamin (b) Hebrew; biblical; 'son of the right hand'. In the Bible, he was the youngest son of Jacob. The name has been used in Britain since the Middle Ages, particularly within the Jewish community, and has recently become especially popular. A 'benjamin' is an old slang term for an overcoat. 'Big Ben' is of course the big bell and clock tower of the Houses of Parliament, named after Sir Benjamin Hall, the Chief Commissioner of Works when the bell was cast. Famous bearers of the name include Benjamin West (1738–1820), the Pennsylvania-born painter.

Berenice (g) Greek; 'victory bringer'. Also **Bernice**.

Bernard (b) German; 'having the courage of a bear'. The name was popularised by several saints especially the theologian St Bernard of Clairvaux (1090–1153), founder of over seventy monasteries. He was also instrumental in persuading the French king Louis VI to undertake the Second Crusade. St Bernard of Menthon was the 'Apostle of the Alps' after whom the alpine passes are named.

Bernarda, Bernadina, Bernadette (g) female forms of Bernard. Bernadette became a common Catholic name after the nineteenth century St Bernadette who saw visions at

Lourdes. The play, *The House of Bernarda Alba*, deals with the family frustrations in a household of girls ruled by their tyrannical mother. It is one of the best-known works by the Spanish poet and dramatist, Federico Garcia Lorca.

Bertha, Berte, Bertha (g) Teutonic; 'bright'. Name of the mother of king Charlemagne and granddaughter of Charles Martel. The name was in vogue throughout Europe during the Middle Ages and was revived in Britain in the nineteenth century. In Dickens' Christmas story, *Cricket on the Hearth*, (1845) Bertha is the blind daughter of Caleb Plummer.

Bertram, Bertrand, Bartram (b) Teutonic; 'bright raven' or 'bright shield'. In Shakespeare's comedy, *All's Well That Ends Well*, Bertram, the Count of Roussillon, is beloved by Helena. The philosopher and mathematician Bertrand Arthur William, 3rd Earl Russell (1872–1970) was a leading pacifist for most of his life and from the late 1940s a champion of nuclear disarmament. In 1949 he gave the first BBC Reith lectures and in 1950 was awarded the Nobel Prize for literature. He wrote his own obituary for *The Times*.

Beryl (g) (occasionally a boy's name). Probably Greek, from the green jewel. The actress Beryl Reid first made her reputation in the radio show, *Educating Archie*. She has appeared in many stage plays including *Entertaining Mr Sloane* (later an acclaimed film), *Blithe Spirit* and *The Way of the World*. Her films include *The Belles of St Trinians* and countless television series.

Bethany (g) Aramaic; 'house of poverty'.

Beverley, Beverly (b) and (g) Perhaps from Old French, 'ox' or from Old English, 'beaver meadow'. It is a modern name, popularized by Beverly Hills in California.

23

Bianca (g) Italian; 'white'. May owe its recent popularity to the glamorous ex-wife of pop singer Mick Jagger.

Björn (b) Old German; 'bear'.

Blair (b) and (g) Gaelic; 'battleground'.

Blake (b) Old English; 'black'.

Blanche (g) French; 'white'. Nowadays less popular than the Italian form **Bianca** and Latin **Candida**. Blanche Dubois, the neurotic central character in Tennesse Williams' play, *A Streetcar Named Desire*, may have influenced the move away from the name.

Bonnie, Bonny (g) Latin; 'good' also Scottish meaning 'looking well'.

Boyd (b) Celtic; 'yellow hair'.

Brad, Bradley (b) Old English; 'broad clearing'.

Brenda (g), **Brendan** (b) Origin uncertain, possibly Old Norse; 'sword'. Popularized by the Irish voyaging saint, St Brendan. The Irish author and playwright Brendan Behan (1923–64), wrote such masterpieces as *The Quare Fellow* and *Borstal Boy*.

Bret, Brett (b) 'from Brittany, Breton'.

Brian, Brien, Bryan (b) Celtic; 'strength'. A particularly popular name in Ireland.

Bridget, Bridgit, Brigid, Brighid, Brigitte (g) St Bridget or St Bride (453–523) is the subject of countless stories concerning her miracles, and Bridget has long been a popular name in Ireland and Scotland. Brigitte Bardot, the French film star and pin-up girl, may be responsible for the naming of some modern-day Brigittes.

Bronwen, Bronwyn (g) Celtic; 'white-breasted'. The name is popular in Wales, where it is connected with legends.

Brook, Brooke (b) and (g) Modern name, probably originating from the surname.

Bruce (b) French. Became popular in the nineteenth century when many Scottish boys were named after King Robert the Bruce (1274–1329) the hero of the Battle of Bannockburn (1314). It was here that 100,000 English soldiers under the leadership of Edward II were routed by Bruce with only 30,000 men.

Bryony (g) From the plant of the same name.

Bunty (g) Perhaps from 'bunny rabbit' or from a pet-name for lambs.

Caleb (b) Hebrew; 'bold'. An Old Testament Biblical name, popular in Britain after the Reformation. The name is commonly found in America and in Scotland.

Calvin (b) Latin 'bald'. Associated with the protestant theologian and reformer John Calvin (1509–64). Calvin Coolidge (1872–1933) was President of the USA from 1923–29.

Camilla, Camille (g) From the Latin; 'attendant at a sacrifice'. It was the name given to the virgin queen of the Volscians. Virgil, *Aeneid vii, 809* says that she was so fleet of foot that she could run across a cornfield without bending a single blade or travel over the sea without even getting her feet wet. The name came into vogue in the eighteenth century, with the taste for the antique. Alexandre Dumas' *La Dame aux Camelias* (published in 1848) about a woman dying of tuberculosis, was a favourite tragic role with many actresses of stage and screen.

Candace, Candice (g) Greek; 'bright white'.

Candida, Candide (g) Latin; 'white'. Candide was the eponymous (male) hero of Voltaire's novel who suffers all kinds of misfortune but remains unaffected by his lot.

Cara, Carina, Carrie (g) Celtic; 'friend'; Italian; 'dear'.

Carl (b) Variant of Charles.

Carla, Carley, Carlotta, Carly (g) variants of **Charlotte**.

Carol (g) and (b), **Carole** (g) Origin uncertain, but probably a form of **Charles**.

Caroline, Carolina (g) Feminine form of Charles, popularized by Caroline of Anspach (1683–1737), queen of George II. Another royal Caroline was the wife of George IV, who is said to have lived a discreditable life at her house on Blackheath. Famous bearers of the name Carolina include Carolina Oliphant, Baroness Nairne (1766–1845) the Scottish songwriter of *Caller Herrin'* among many other songs. There are many variants, including **Carolyn, Carlene, Charleen** and **Sharlene**.

Catharine, Catherine (g) Greek; 'pure'. The name of a much-loved saint, St Catharine of Alexandria, the patron saint of girls. She was a beautiful and intelligent virgin of noble descent, who was tortured by being bound between spiked wheels. She was then beheaded. The fourteenth century St Catharine of Sienna, a Dominican, was chosen by the Florentines to intercede with Pope Gregory XI on their behalf, and she persuaded him to return from Avignon to Rome. The ambitious queen, Catharine de Medici (1519–59), was the wife of the French king Henry II and mother of three monarchs, Francis II, Charles IX and Henry III. Three different Catharines were wives of the notorious Henry VIII – Catharine of Aragon, Catharine Howard and Catharine Parr. Catharine was also the name of two Russian empresses, Catharine I (1684–1727), the orphaned daughter of a Lithuanian peasant who in 1725 married Peter the Great, and Catharine II 'the Great' (1729–96). The name can also be spelt with a K and there are many variants including **Caitlin, Caterina, Cathrine, Catriona, Kathlene, Katy, Katya.**

Cecil (b) (formerly, and occasionally, also [g]) Latin; 'blind'. Cecil Rhodes (1853–1902) made his fortune from diamond mining in South Africa. He then became Prime Minister of the Cape Colony and extended British territory in what was to become known as Rhodesia (now Zimbabwe). Cecil Sharp (1859–1924) was the London-born collector of folk songs and dances.

Cecilia, Cecile, Cecily (g) Feminine forms of Cecil. Cecilia owes its popularity to the third-century virgin saint, reputed to be so close to heaven that she could hear the angels singing. She was also said to have invented the organ and is the patron saint of musicians. Recent Cecilias may be named after the song by songwriters Simon and Garfunkel.

Chantal, Chantel, Chantalle (g) From the French.

Charles (b) Teutonic; 'man'. Extremely popular in its various translated forms throughout medieval Europe. There have been many royal bearers of the name including Charlemagne or Charles the Great (742–814), king of the Franks and the first Holy Emperor, who helped to spread learning and com-

28

merce throughout his vast empire. There were two kings of Great Britain and Ireland, Charles I (1600–49), tried for treason and executed in front of Whitehall; and Charles II (1630–85), said by Defoe to have had 'a world of wit and not a grain of ill-nature in him'. Ten kings of France were called Charles, including Charles the Bald, Charles the Fat and Charles the Foolish (the name has remained popular despite these!) and seven Holy Roman Emperors including Charlemagne. There were four kings of Spain; fifteen kings of Sweden and kings of Sardinia, Naples and Sicily as well as dukes, emperors and princes, amongst whom is the present heir to the British throne (born in 1948).

Charlotte (g) French feminine form of **Charles** made fashionable by Charlotte Sophia (1744–1818) the wife of George III, her eldest daughter, Charlotte Augusta Matilda, and by the much-loved and tragic Princess Charlotte (1796–1817). She was the daughter of the future George IV who after only eighteen months of marriage to Prince Leopold of Saxe-Coburg died at the age of 21 giving birth to a stillborn son. Another Charlotte was one of the three distinguished Brontë sisters who were all great writers. Charlotte's famous masterpiece is *Jane Eyre*.

Charmaine (g) Perhaps a variant of Charmian, from the Greek 'source of charm' and the name of Cleopatra's handmaiden.

Chere, Cher, Cherie (g) French; 'dear', 'darling'. Variants include **Cherry, Sherry, Sher**.

29

Chloe (g) Greek; 'green, summery'. The name has been in use for four centuries and is becoming increasingly popular with modern parents. In mythology, Chloe was the shepherdess whom Daphnis loved.

Christabel (g) Latin; 'beautiful annointed one'. Has been in use since the Middle Ages. The famous suffragette Christabel Pankhurst (1880–1958) is perhaps one of the most well-known bearers of the name.

Christian (b) Latin; 'follower of Christ'. This is the name given to many Scandinavian kings including Christian IV (1577–1648), king of Denmark and Norway and Duke of Schleswig-Holstein, hero of the ballad *King Christian stood by the lofty mast*. The great French medieval poet Chretien de Troyes (died *c.* 1183) was the author of Arthurian romances.

Christina, Christine, Christiana, Christina (g) Female forms of Christian. Christine de Pisan (*c.* 1363–1431), born in Venice and raised in Paris, supported her children by her writing, including love poems and an educational compendium for women. Queen Christina of Sweden (1626–89) is probably best-known outside her native land from the historically inaccurate 1933 film which starred Greta Garbo. Variants and diminutives of Christine, which has been in use since the eleventh century, include **Christy, Chrissie, Chris, Kirstin, Kirsty, Kristina** and **Tina**, which are all used as names in their own right.

Christmas (b) and (g) Hardly surprising this name is sometimes used for children born on Christmas Day.

Christopher (b) Greek; 'bearer of Christ'. A name popular since medieval times, because of the cult of the third-century martyr, patron saint of travellers, said to have carried the infant Christ across a ford. The great English architect Sir Christopher Wren (1632–1723) designed St Paul's Cathedral and more than fifty other London churches to replace those lost in the Great Fire of 1666. Twenty-three of these beautiful churches still survive. Amazingly, apart from his work on the new St Paul's, Christopher Wren was given no formal payment for any of his designs. Modern-day Christophers include the English dramatist Christopher Fry, author of *The Lady's not for Burning* (1949) and *The Dark is Light Enough* (1954) and Christopher Isherwood who wrote *Goodbye to Berlin* (1939), on which book the musical *Cabaret* was based.

Chrystal, Crystal (g) a jewel name.

Clair, Claire, Clare, Clara (g) Latin; 'bright, clear'. The name was given to the thirteenth-century saint, who was a disciple of St Francis of Assisi. She founded, with St Francis, the order of Franciscan nuns called the 'Poor Clares' whose main work was the education and welfare of poor girls. She died in 1253 and was canonized two years later. In 1958 she was made patron saint of television because she is said to have seen and heard a Christmas service taking place in Assisi while in her cell at the Convent of San Damiano. The name Clare has been popular in England since her death, the form Clara came into favour in the nineteenth century. Clara Schumann (1819–96) the German composer and leading concert pianist; and Clara Bow (1905–1965) the American film star who was a great hit in films depicting the flapper generation, are amongst those given the name.

31

Clarence (b), **Clarice, Clarissa** (g) Latin; 'being renowned'. Male and female variants of the name Clare. Clarissa is one of the main characters in *The Confederacy*, a comedy by Vanbrugh, which was produced in 1705. *Clarissa Harlowe* is a novel by Richardson (1689–1761), in which the heroine Clarissa's story is related through a series of letters.

Clark, Clarke (b) From the surname, meaning a person who was able to read and write, usually a clergyman, since in early times they were responsible for all written business transactions. The American actor Clark Gable (born William Clark Gable) (1901–1960), a film star for some thirty years, helped to popularize the name in this century.

Claud, Claude (b), **Claudia, Claudine, Claudette** (g) Latin; 'lame'. Derives from the name Claudius. Both the male and female forms have been used in one version or another in England since the first century AD. The seventeenth-century French landscape painter, Claude Lorraine, lived and worked in Italy for most of his life. The *Claudine* series of novels was written by the French author Colette (1873–1954).

Clement (b), **Clementine, Clemence, Clementina** (g) Latin; 'merciful'. St Clement of Rome (second century) was one of the earliest bishops of Rome and a renowned Christian writer. Clement Attlee (1883–1967) the English Labour statesman and Clementine Churchill, wife of Sir Winston, are among some other recent bearers of the name.

Clifford (b) Teutonic; 'dweller on a slope'. The diminutive, Cliff, has been given some popularity by Cliff Richard.

Clive (b) A contraction of Clifford, it owes its popularity to Robert Clive — Clive of India, the eighteenth-century soldier and administrator.

Clodagh (g) Irish; the name of a river in Tipperary.

Colette (g) French; diminutive of **Nicole**. Sidonie Gabrielle Colette (1873–1954) was the author of *Cheri*, *La Chatte* and *Gigi* among many other novels. Two films have been based on *Gigi*, the more famous being the 1958 Lerner and Loewe musical which won nine Academy Awards.

Colin (b) Latin; 'a dove'.

Colleen (g) Old Irish; 'girl'.

Conal, Connal, Connel (b) Irish, from the Celtic; 'high-mighty'.

Conan (b) Celtic; 'wise'. Sir Arthur Conan Doyle (1859–1930), the creator of the detective Sherlock Holmes and his friend Dr Watson, had this unusual name. He was also the author of historical romances and wrote on spiritualism.

Conor (b) Irish, from Celtic; 'high desire'. A popular Irish name.

Constant (b) Derives from the adjective. The composer Constant Lambert (1905–51) was associated with Sadler's Wells Ballet. His most successful works include *Pomona* and *Horoscope*.

Constance, (g) Latin; 'firm of purpose'. The name has been known in Britain since Norman times.

Constantine (b) Made famous by the Roman Emperor Constantine the Great (*c.* 274–337) who by the Edict of Milan granted toleration to Christianity throughout the Roman Empire. He chose Byzantium as his capital and named it Constantinople ('City of Constantine').

Corin (b), **Cora, Corinna** (g) Greek; 'maiden'. Corinna, the Greek lyric poet, is said to have instructed the young poet Pindar, advising him to sow his mythological detail 'by the handful, not by the sackful'. She was said to have won five victories over him in poetic contests.

Cordelia (g) Celtic; 'daughter of the sea'. In Shakespeare's *King Lear* the king's youngest and only faithful daughter.

Cornelia (g), **Cornelius** (b) Latin; 'regal'.

Craig (b) Celtic; 'rugged rock'.

Crispin, Crispian (b) Latin; 'curly haired'. St Crispin (martyred 287) is, jointly with his brother, the patron saint of shoemakers. The name was most popular during the Middle Ages.

Curtis (b) Origin uncertain. Possibly Middle English; 'short hose' or Old French; 'courteous'.

Daisy (g) Anglo-Saxon; *daeges eage*, 'eye of day', so named from the flower which covers its yellow disk in the evening and reveals it again in the morning. Popularized by the song 'Daisy, Daisy, give me your answer do', a nineteenth-century favourite.

Dale (b) and (g) Anglo-Saxon; 'dweller in a valley'.

Damian (b) Greek; 'tamer'. Third-century saint who, with his brother Cosmas, devoted his life to medicine and surgery — they are both patron saints. They were also adopted as patron saints by the wealthy Florentine family, the Medicis.

Damon (b) Variant of the above. Damon and Phintias (or Pythias) were two Pythagoreans of Syracuse renowned for their close friendship. Phintias was condemned to death by Dionysius I, but arranged to go off and put his affairs in order leaving Damon in his place to die if he failed to return. He returned to be executed before his time had expired, so impressing Dionysius that he freed them and asked to become the friend of both of them. (Alfred) Damon Runyon (1884–1946) the Kansas-born author and journalist, is particularly known for his short stories of the gangsters, crooks and bootleggers of Broadway, New York, written in the present tense and spiced with the current American slang. The 1955 musical film *Guys and Dolls* starring Frank Sinatra, Marlo Brando, Jean Simmons, Vivian Blane and Stubby Kaye, was based on one of his stories.

Dane (b) Old Norse: 'Dane, native of Denmark'.

Daniel, (b) **Danielle** (g) Hebrew; 'judged of God'. Biblical prophet. The name was commonly used during the Reformation, when Old Testament names came into fashion. It has long been a popular name, especially in Ireland. Diminutives include Dan and Danny. The song *Danny Boy* is a well-known Irish favourite. The American pioneer Daniel Boone (1735–1820) lived in the forest and was twice captured by Indians.

Dante (b) From the Italian. The poet Dante Alighieri (1265–1321) was baptized Durante, 'lasting', afterwards contracted to Dante 'the giver'. His great works are the *Vita Nuova* and the *Divina Commedia*, which tell of his love for Beatrice. The romantic associations of the name made it popular in England in the Middle Ages and again during the nineteenth-century medieval revival. Dante Gabriel Rossetti (1828–82) the poet and painter drew his subjects mainly from Dante and the medieval world.

Daphne (g) Greek; 'bay-tree, laurel'. In classical mythology Daphne is the daughter of a river god. When pursued by Apollo she was changed into a laurel, which afterwards became Apollo's favourite tree.

Darrell, Daryl (b) and **Darlene, Darelle** (g) Anglo-Saxon; from 'darling'.

Darren (b) origin uncertain, perhaps from Darius, or from a surname. A name which has become popular in the second half of the twentieth century.

David (b) Hebrew; biblical; 'beloved'. In the Bible, the youngest son of Jesse of Bethlehem who slayed Goliath, later became king of Judah and went on to rule all Israel, conquering Jerusalem and making it the religious and political centre of his kingdom. The patron saint of Wales is St David (or St Dewi), a tenth-century bishop who presided over two Welsh Synods. Two kings of Scotland were also Davids. David I (1080–1153) helped to unite the different races of Scotland into one nation. David II (1324–71), the son of Robert the Bruce, invaded England but was defeated and imprisoned for eleven years. David is one of the favourite boys' names, particularly this century.

Davida, Davina (g) English and Scottish feminine forms of David.

Dawn (g) English 'daybreak'.

Dean (b) surname, Old English; 'one who lives in a valley'. Popularized in this century by the American actor, Dean Martin and the politician Dean Rusk, who played a prominent role in the 1962 Cuban crisis. James Dean (1931–1955), film star of the fifties films *East of Eden*, *Rebel without a Cause* and *Giant*, whose untimely death in a car crash turned him into a cult figure, is still popular today.

Deanna (g) variant of **Diana**. Popularized earlier this century by the Canadian film star, Deanna Durbin.

Deborah (g) Hebrew; biblical; 'eloquent'. This name was favoured by the Puritans in seventeenth-century England. Variants and diminutives include **Debra**, **Deb**, **Debbie**, **Debby**.

Deirdre (g) Celtic; 'raging one'. Name of one of the great heroines of Ireland and popularized by Irish poetry.

Delia (g) Greek; from the island of Delos, birthplace of the goddess Artemis (Diana).

Denis, Dennis, Denys (b), **Denise** (g) Greek; contraction of Dionysos, god of wine. St Denis, the third-century martyr was the first bishop of Paris. The name was brought to Britain by the Normans.

Denzil (b) From a sixteenth-century Cornish family name.

Derek, Deric, Derick, Derrick (b) Teutonic; 'people's wealth' or 'people's ruler'. Although found in Britain since the fifteenth century it has only been popular during the twentieth. The respected British actor Derek Jacobi (1939–   ) is most famous for his portrayal of Claudius in the television adaptation of Robert Graves' *I Claudius* and *Claudius the God*.

Dermot, Diarmid (b) Celtic; 'free from envy'. Very popular Irish name.

Desirée (g) French; 'desired'.

Desmond (b) Celtic; originally a clan-name, meaning 'from South Munster'.

38

Diana, Diane, Dyan, Dyana (g) Latin; 'the bright one'. Name of the Roman goddess of light, chastity, hunting and the moon and a fertility goddess. Diana became a fashionable name in Britain in the eighteenth century and its popularity has recently been increased by the marriage of the heir to the throne, Prince Charles, to Lady Diana Spencer.

Dilys (g) Welsh; 'perfect'.

Dionne, Dione (g) From the Greek. Mother of Aphrodite by Zeus.

Dirk (b) Teutonic; 'people's ruler'. The actor Dirk Bogarde (Derek Van Den Bogaerd) has appeared in numerous films including *Doctor in the House, A Tale of Two Cities* and *Death in Venice*.

Dominic (b), **Dominica, Dominique** (g) Latin; 'born on the Lord's day'. Originally given to children born on a Sunday, the masculine version, especially, is now popular, particularly amongst Roman Catholics. St Dominic (thirteenth century) born at Calahorra in Spain, was the founder of the Order of Preachers which became the Dominican Order. He died at Bologna in 1221.

Donald (b) Gaelic; 'ruler of the world'. Mainly Scottish, brought into favour by royal connections. Donald Campbell (1921–67) broke the world water speed record on Ullswater in 1955 and continued to break his own record, reaching 276.33 mph in Australia in 1964. Pet forms of the name include **Don** and **Donny**.

Donna (g) Italian; 'lady'.

Donovan (b) Old Irish; 'dark warrior'.

39

Doran (b) Greek; 'gift'.

Dorian (b) Greek; place name.

Dorinda (g) In the verses of the Earl of Dorset, Dorinda was Catherine Sedley, Countess of Dorchester, the mistress of James II.

Doris (g) Greek; meaning obscure, possibly 'of the sea'. In Greek mythology, the daughter of Oceanus by Thetis; wife of Nereus and mother of the Nereids.

Dorothea, Dorothy, Dorothee, Doreen (g) Greek; 'a gift of God'. St Dorothea of Cappadocia, a third-century martyr, first popularized the name. In this century many girls have been named after the heroine, Dorothy, from *The Wizard of Oz*. Famous authors called Dorothy include Dorothy Parker (1893–1967) the American writer, known for her acid wit; Dorothy L. Sayers (1893–1957) the English detective story writer, creator of Lord Peter Wimsey; and the author of the *Pilgrimage* novels, Dorothy Miller (1873–1957).

Dougal (b) Old Irish; 'dark stranger'.

Douglas (b) Gaelic; 'dark stream'. Scottish clan-name.

Drew (b) Teutonic; 'bearer'.

Dudley (b) Popularized by Sir Robert Dudley (1573–1649).

Duncan (b) Gaelic; 'brown warrior'. Popular Scottish name. The Scottish king, Duncan I, was killed in 1040 by Macbeth, as recounted in Shakespeare's play. Duncan Sandys, the British Conservative politician, adopted, as

Minister of Defence, a controversial cost-cutting programme for the Forces.

Dunstan (b) Anglo-Saxon; 'hill-stone'. Made popular by the English St Dunstan (909–88), Archbishop of Canterbury, and a religious reformer and royal adviser.

Dustin (b) Meaning unknown. The actor Dustin Hoffman won an Oscar for his performance in *Rainman* (1989).

Dwayne, Duane (b) From a surname. Irish.

Dwight (b) Derived from a surname now used in the USA as a first name. Dwight Eisenhower (1890–1969), the American general and 34th President, is probably the most famous person with this name.

Dylan (b) Welsh; 'the sea'. Recent Dylans were probably named after the Swansea-born poet Dylan Thomas (1914–53), author of many works including *Portrait of the Artist as a Young Dog* and *Under Milk Wood*, or the singer and songwriter Bob Dylan (who took his own stage name from the Welsh poet).

Eamon (b) Irish form of Edmund.

Earl (b) Old English; 'a noble'.

Ebony (g) Old Norse; 'work'. Also the hard black wood and thus 'black'.

Edgar (b) Anglo-Saxon; 'fortunate spear'. Edgar Wallace (1875–1932) the journalist, novelist and playwright, adapted many of his crime novels for the stage.

Edmond, Edmund (b) Anglo-Saxon; 'happy protector'. The name was made popular by St Edmund (*c.* 841–870), king of East Anglia, defeated and shot to death with arrows during the Danish invasion, because he refused to give up his faith. Royal associations were strengthened by Edmund King of the English (*c.* 922–946) and by Edmund Ironside (*c.* 981–1016) the English king who fought against Canute.

They eventually reached a compromise and the country was divided between Canute and Edmund, the survivor to succeed to the whole. Only a few weeks after this, Edmund died.

Sir Edmund Hillary, the New Zealand mountaineer and explorer, reached the summit of Mount Everest in May 1953 helped by Sherpa Tensing. For this feat he received a knighthood.

Edward (b) Anglo-Saxon; 'rich guardian'. A name in constant use from Saxon times, the name of three English Saxon kings, Edward the Elder, Edward the Martyr and Edward the Confessor (canonized in 1161). Eight post-Conquest monarchs bore the name, the last, Edward VIII, abdicating in 1936, after less than a year's reign, following the crisis over his wish to marry Mrs Ernest Simpson. Edward the Black Prince (1330–76), the son of Edward III, was a great soldier, fighting at Crécy, Poitiers and Navarrete.

Edward Heath (1916–), was educated at Balliol College, Oxford, where he read PPE and won an organ scholarship. He served in the Royal Artillery during World War II and entered Parliament in 1950. He became Conservative Prime Minister in 1970. Diminutives of Edward include **Ed, Eddie, Eddy, Ted, Teddy**.

Edwin (b) Old English; 'rich friend, happy friend'. Royal and saint's name. St Edwin (585–633), king of Northumbria, subdued the whole of England except Kent. The name was revived in the nineteenth century.

Edwina (g) Female form of the above.

Eileen (g) Irish form of Helen, sometimes spelt **Aileen**.

Elaine (g) Variant of Helen.

Eleanor, Eleanora, Eleanore, Elinor, Ellenor (and other variants) (g) forms of Helen. The name Eleanor was introduced to England by Eleanor of Aquitaine (*c.* 1122–1204), wife of Henry II and further popularized by Queen Eleanor of Provence, wife of Henry III of England and by Eleanor of Castile. The latter, the first wife of Edward I, accompanied him on the crusades and is reputed to have saved his life by sucking out the poison from a wound. She died in 1290 in Nottinghamshire and Edward erected 'Eleanor crosses' at the nine places where her cortege rested. The last stopping place was Charing Cross in London, where a replica memorial cross can be seen outside the mainline railway station. Three original crosses still stand at Northampton, Geddington and Waltham Cross, Essex.

Eli (b) Hebrew; 'exalted'. Old Testament name.

Elias (b) Hebrew; 'Jehovah is God'. Also **Ellis**.

Eliot, Elliot, Ellis (b) From the surnames, or variants of **Eli, Elijah** and **Elisha**.

Elizabeth, Elisabeth (g) Hebrew; 'oath of God'. One of the most popular girls' names, introduced to England in the fifteenth century by Queen Elizabeth I (1533–1603) who made the name a favourite. The name has numerous diminutives and variants including **Bess, Bessy, Bet, Beth, Betsy, Bettina, Betty, Elsbet, Elspeth, Elsa, Lilibeth, Lilibet, Lisbeth, Liz, Lizzy, Lizzie, Liza, Eliza, Lisa, Elisa, Lise, Lil, Lily, Lilly, Lillie.**

Ellen (g) Scottish variant of Helen.

Elmer (b) Anglo-Saxon; 'noble'. A derivative of Aylmer.

44

Eloise (g) Feminine derivative of Louis; 'famous war'. Also spelt Heloise.

Elroy (b) Spanish; 'king'.

Elsa (g) German derivative of Elizabeth.

Elspeth (g) Scottish; contraction of Elizabeth.

Elvira, Elvire (g) Old German: 'elf counsel'. Literary: Elvira was the wife of Don Juan, according to the Spanish story; the heroine of John Dryden's *The Spanish Fryar* (1681), an attack on the papists. She was also the mistress of Pizarro in Sheridan's play of the same name (1799), the heroine of Victor Hugo's *Hernani* and the deceased first wife in *Blithe Spirit* (1941) by Noel Coward.

Elvis (b) Old Norse; 'all wise'.

Emerald, Esmeralda (g) One of the jewel names, fashionable at the end of the 19th century.

Emil, Emile (b), **Emily, Emilie, Emilia, Emmeline, Emmelina, Amelia** (g) Old French; 'industrious'. Emilia was the lady beloved by Palamon and Arcite, the Emelye of *the Knight's Tale* in Chaucer's *Canterbury Tales*. 'Little Emily' appears in Charles Dickens' *David Copperfield*.

Emlyn (b) Welsh; 'work serpent'. Emlyn Williams, the Welsh playwright numbers amongst his successes *Night Must Fall* (1935), a chilling murder story; *The Corn is Green* and *Trespass*. Also an accomplished actor, he will be remembered for his solo performance as Charles Dickens.

Emma (g) Teutonic; contraction of Ermentrude. Used in Britain since Norman times. *Emma* (1814–1816) the novel by Jane Austen, tells the story of Emma and the pretty, but foolish, Harriet on whose behalf Emma devises schemes to effect a marriage with various eligible young men.

Emmanuel, Emanuel (b) Hebrew; 'God with us'. This has always been a popular name within the Jewish community. Emanuel 'Manny' Shinwell (1884–1986), the British Labour politician, nationalized the coal mines in 1946 as minister of fuel and power, became secretary of state for war and from 1950–51 was minister of defence.

Ena (g) Origin uncertain, perhaps from Greek; 'praise'. A name more recently popularized by the character, Ena Sharples, in the television series, *Coronation Street.*

Enid (g) Celtic; 'spotless purity'. In Arthurian legend Enid is the wife of Prince Geraint, one of the Knights of the Round Table, and known as 'Enid the Fair' and 'Enid the Good'. The name became fashionabl during the nineteenth-century medieval revival, greatly helped by *Geraint and Enid*, one of Tennyson's *Idylls of the King* (1859).

Ephraim (b) Hebrew; biblical; 'fruitful'. One of the sons of Joseph in the Bible. A popular name in the USA.

Eric (b) Norse; 'ever king'. Name of several Swedish and Danish kings. Eric the Red, a Norwegian sailor, the subject of various Icelandic sagas, explored the coast of Greenland and founded colonies there. The composer Erik Satie (1866–1925) is known for his ballet music.

Erica (g) Feminine form of Eric.

Erin, Erinna (g) Old Irish; 'peace'.

Ernest (b) Teutonic; 'grave, serious'. Sir Ernest Shackleton (1874–1922) made several expeditions to the Antarctic. On one of these, in 1915, his ship *Endeavour* was crushed in the ice and Shackleton and his men made a heroic escape by sledges and boats.

Ernestine (g) Feminine form of Ernest.

Errol (b) Latin; 'wanderer'. Errol Flynn (1909–1959), the Tasmanian-born screen hero, will be remembered for such films as *The Adventures of Robin Hood* and *They died with their boots on.*

Esme (b) and (g) French; 'esteemed'.

Esmond, Esmund (b) Teutonic; 'divine protection, divine protector'.

Estelle, Estella (g) from the French; 'star'. In Dickens' *Great Expectations* Estella is the beautiful girl with whom the hero Pip falls in love.

Esther (g) Persian; biblical, also literary; 'star'. Also spelt Hester. Esther Lyon is the heroine of George Eliot's novel *Felix Holt* published in 1866. Esther Summerson appears in Dickens' *Bleak House*, and *Esther Waters* (1894) is a novel by the Anglo-Irish writer George Moore.

Eugene (b) Greek; 'well-born'. Often shortened to Gene. Eugene O'Neill (1888–1953), the American playwright, the son of an actor, started to write when recovering in a sanitorium from tuberculosis. His most famous plays are probably *Mourning Becomes Electra* (1931) a version of the *Oresteia*; *The Ice Man Cometh* and *Long Day's Journey into Night*. In 1936 O'Neill was awarded the Nobel Prize for Literature. Gene Pitney was a successful pop singer in the 1960s.

Eugenia, Eugenie (g) Feminine form of the above. Popularized by Eugenie de Montijo, a Spanish countess, who in January 1853 married Napoleon III in the cathedral of Notre Dame. Though the match was an unpopular one, Eugenie is said to have won people's affection by her beauty, sweetness and charm. After the Emperor's surrender at Sedan she fled to England where in March 1871 Napoleon joined her. They lived in Chislehurst, Kent. Recently popularized by Princess Eugenie.

Eunice (g) Greek; 'happy victory', 'wife'. Favoured in the seventeenth century by the Puritans.

Euphemia (g) Greek; 'auspicious speech'. Diminutives include **Effie**.

Eustace (b) Greek; 'happy harvest'. St Eustace was a second-century Christian martyr. *The Eustace Diamonds* (1873) by Anthony Trollope tells of family quarrels to possess a diamond necklace.

Eva, Eve (g) Hebrew; biblical; 'life'. In the Bible, Eve is the name of the first woman God created. Found in Britain since the twelfth century.

Evan (b) Celtic; 'young warrior', also a Welsh form of *John*. Variants include **Euan, Ewen** and **Ewan**. *Evan Harrington*

(1861), the story of a tailor's son, was written by George Meredith, himself the grandson of a wealthy Portsmouth tailor and naval outfitter.

Evangeline (g) Greek; 'happy messenger', from the heroine of a narrative poem by Longfellow, published in 1847. The poem tells of the expulsion of the peasants of Arcadia from their homes during which the lovers Evangeline and Gabriel are separated for years. It tells of the search by Evangeline for Gabriel, who she eventually is reunited with in an almshouse just before he dies.

Evelyn (g) and, less usually (b). Possibly Celtic; 'pleasant', or Old German, meaning uncertain. One of the stock names introduced to Britain by the Normans. Other feminine forms include **Evelyne**, **Eveline** and **Evelina** — popularized by the novel by Fanny Burney, published in 1778. Evelyn Waugh (1903–66) who wrote such novels as *Black Mischief*, *Scoop* and *Brideshead Revisited*, had a wife called Evelyn.

Ezra (b) Hebrew; 'help'.

Fabian, Fabius (b), **Fabia** (g) Latin; 'bean-grower'. Fabius was the name of one of the most ancient and distinguished patrician families in Rome. Members of the family included generals, the earliest known Roman historian, consuls and an artist who painted the earliest known Roman paintings on the temple of Salus.

Faith (g) Derived from the Latin; '*fides*', this is one of the abstract 'virtue' names which were favoured by the Puritans in the sixteenth and seventeenth centuries. *Fides Publica* was a Roman goddess who represented the honour of the people. Sacrifices were made to her each year on 1st October. Variants include **Fay, Faye. Faythe**.

Fanny (g) Diminutive of Frances.

Fatima (g) Arabic; 'daughter of the Prophet'.

Farquhar (b) Gaelic; 'friendly man'. Almost exclusively Scottish.

Farrer (b) and (g) Latin; 'iron, blacksmith'.

Felicia, Felicity (g), **Felix** (b) Latin; 'happiness'. Felix was the name of numerous early saints and is also used to mean a member of the cat family. The cartoon character, Felix the Cat, created by Pat Sullivan, was popular with cinema audiences in the 1920s.

Fenella (g) Old Irish; 'white-shouldered'.

Fenton (b) Old English; 'marshy town'. Possibly from a surname.

Ferdinand (b) Teutonic; 'venturous life'. Used from the Middle Ages and a name favoured and popularized by European royalty throughout the centuries.

Fergus (b) Celtic; 'man's strength'. Popular amongst Irish and Scottish communities. Variants include **Feargus**.

Fern (g) Sanskrit; 'feather'.

Fidel (b), **Fidelia** (g) Latin; 'faithful'.

Fingal (b) Celtic; 'fair stranger'. Fingal's Cave is an enormous natural cavern in the isle of Staffa, described in *Lord of the Isles* by Sir Walter Scott and the subject of Felix Mendelssohn's concert overture *The Hebrides* which was inspired by his visit to the Western Isles of Scotland. Fingal himself is the hero of several Ossianic poems.

Fiona, Finella, Fionola, Fionnuala, Fionnula, Fenella (g) Celtic; 'white girl'. Fiona Macleod was a pseudonym of the Scottish writer William Sharp (1855–1905) under which he wrote Celtic mystical prose and verse. He may actually have invented the name Fiona. Sharp refused to acknowledge his pen name of Fiona Macleod and it was only confirmed after his death, although he wrote biographies of contemporary poets and volumes of poetry under his own name. The legendary Fionnuala, subject of one of Moore's *Irish Melodies*, is changed into a swan and condemned to wander over the Irish waters until Christianity came to Ireland.

Flavia (g), **Flavian**, **Flavius** (b) Latin; 'golden'.

Fletcher (b) Old French; 'maker or dealer in bows and arrows', 'one who fits arrows with feathers'. Fletcher Christian was the ringleader of the famous mutiny on board the ship *HMS Bounty* in 1789. Christian and others seized Lt. Bligh, the commander, and cast him and eighteen members of his crew adrift in an open boat.

Fleur (g) French; **Flora** (g) Latin; 'flower'. Flora was the Roman goddess of flowers. Her festival, the Floralia, first instituted in 238 BC and celebrated from time to time became an annual event after 173 BC. It lasted from 28th April to 3rd May and featured licentious stage exhibitions. Flora Macdonald (1722–90) was the Scottish heroine who is said to have helped the Young Pretender 'Bonnie Prince Charlie' escape. She disguised him as a woman, and took him from Benbecula to Portree in June 1746. Flora Thompson (1876–1947) was the author of the autobiographical chronicles of life in Victorian rural Oxfordshire *Lark Rise*, *Over to Candleford*, *Candleford Green* and *Still Glides the Stream*. The French version of the name was brought into vogue by John Galsworthy in his series of novels known as *The Forsyte Saga*. Other variants of the name include **Fleurette**, **Florrie**, **Flore**, **Florinda**.

Florence (g) Latin; 'blooming'. The chief city of Tuscany, Italy, a cradle of the Renaissance. Florence Nightingale (1820–1910), the English hospital reformer, known as the 'lady with the lamp', was born in Florence and named after it.

Florinda (g) Literary from **Flora**. Florinda appears in Robert Southey's *Roderick the Last of the Goths* (1814).

Floyd (b) From the surname Lloyd. The American bantamweight boxer, Floyd Favors (1963–   ) has achieved success in the World Championships though his domestic record has been less successful.

Frances, Francesca, Françoise (g), **Francis** (b) Latin, 'free', 'a Frenchman'. Royal and saints names. The history of Francesca da Rimini, who loved her husband's brother, and who in 1285 was killed with her lover by her husband, is incorporated in Dante's *Inferno*. St Francesca Xavier Cabrini (1850–1917), was born in Italy but emigrated to the USA in 1887, and became the first American saint.

Francis is the name of four saints of which the most famous are St Francis of Assisi and St Francis Xavier. St Francis of Assisi is said to have acquired the name Francesco, 'the Frenchman' because he had learned French in his youth and loved the Provençal troubadour ballads. At the age of 24 he decided to devote his life to God and by 1210 he had a brotherhood of eleven who became the first Franciscans. His day is 4th October, the day on which he died in 1226. St Francis Xavier was associated with Loyola in founding the Jesuit Society in 1534. His missionary journeys included visits to Goa, Malacca, Sri Lanka and Japan. Francis was also the name of two kings of France and of two Holy Roman Emperors as well as of other titled

53

heads of Europe. Sir Francis Drake (*c*. 1540–96), the great Elizabethan seaman, made the name popular in the sixteenth century. The British yachtsman, Francis Chichester (1901–72), made in 1966–67 a solo circumnavigation of the world in *Gipsy Moth IV* and was knighted at Greenwich, London, with Sir Francis Drake's sword.

There are many variants of both Frances and Francis including, for girls, **Fran**, **Franny**, **France**, **Francine** and **Frankie** (popularized by the black American ballad in which Frankie shoots her lover to avenge the wrong he has done her). For boys, variants include **Frank**. Many recent Franks may have been named after the famous singer and actor, Frank Sinatra. Frank was also the name of the founder of F. W. Woolworth, the famous chain store. **Franklin** (as in Franklin Delano Roosevelt, 32nd President of the USA) and **Franklyn** are other variants.

Fraser, Frazer (b) Possibly from the surname.

Freda, Frida, Frieda (g) From Winifred, Celtic; 'white wave' or German; 'peace'.

Frederick, Frederic (b), **Frederica** (g) Old German; 'peaceful ruler'. The name of three Holy Roman Emperors, three Prussian kings, nine Danish kings and various other members of European royalty, some of whom have been by no means 'peaceful rulers'. Perhaps the most illustrious of all was Frederick the Great of Prussia (1712–86), though it was Frederick, Prince of Wales (1707–51), the son of George II and father of George III who is mainly responsible for bringing the name into favour in England.

Gabriel (b), **Gabriela**, **Gabriella**, **Gabrielle**, **Gabie** (g)
Hebrew; 'man of God'; biblical. Gabriel was one of the four
archangels who appears in the Book of Daniel and in St
Luke's Gospel in which he announces to Mary the future
birth of Jesus. This scene, the Annunciation, was a favourite
subject of Renaissance art where Gabriel is generally
depicted holding a lily.

In the Muslim religion, Gabriel is also one of the four
principal angels. The name was common in Britain during
the Middle Ages. Gabrielle Réjane, the Parisian comedy
actress, performed frequently in London and appeared in
New York in 1895 in the title role of Sardou's *Madame
Sans-Gêne*. Gabriel Fauré (1845–1924) the French
composer, organist and teacher, influenced his contem-
poraries including Ravel. He is chiefly remembered for his
chansons (songs) and Requiem.

Gail (g) Origin uncertain, possibly a diminutive of **Abigail**
or from Old German; 'lofty'. Gayle is also found.

Gareth, Garreth, Gary, Garry, Garth (b) Gareth is an old Welsh name revived by Tennyson's *Gareth and Lynette*, one of the *Idylls of the King* published in 1872. Gary, the 'diminutive', was popularized by Gary Cooper (1901–1961) (real name Frank J. Cooper) the tall, slow-speaking American star of romances, comedies and adventure films, particularly westerns.

Garth (b) Welsh; 'highland'.

Gemma (g) Italian; 'precious stone'. Gemma Craven has appeared in many stage shows, films and TV series.

Gene (b) and (g) Greek; 'nobly born'.

Gay, Gaye (g) From the adjective.

Gemma (g) Italian; 'precious stone'. Gemma Craven (born 1950 in Dublin) has appeared in many stage shows, films and TV series.

Genevieve (g) Latin; 'fair girl'. Patron saint of Paris. The 1954 British comedy film *Genevieve* centres on a car race.

Geoffrey (b) Teutonic; 'God's peace'. Also spelt Jeffrey. Geoffrey of Monmouth (1100?–1154), a Benedictine monk, was a 'historian' whose *Historia Regum Britanniae* has greatly influenced English literature. He created the legend of King Arthur as a romantic hero. Geoffrey Chaucer (*c.* 1345–1400) combined a career as a soldier, secret agent, diplomat and controller of customs with that of the first great — perhaps the greatest ever — English poet. His works include *Troilus and Cressida* and *The Canterbury Tales*. He was the first poet to be buried in what became known as Poet's Corner in Westminster Abbey. Diminutives are **Geoff, Jeff**.

George (b), **Georgia, Georgina, Georgiana** (g) Greek; 'farmer'. St George is the patron saint of England (saint's day 23rd April), guardian of Portugal, formerly patron of Aragon and Genoa, patron of the Italian cities of Ferrara and Venice, patron of chivalry, soldiers and armorers. He is the subject of many different legends, including the tale of him slaying a fierce dragon. Very little is known of him factually, however. His cult was especially popular at the time of the Crusades. St George was one of the best-loved subjects of Renaissance artists where he is usually depicted as a young knight in armour emblazoned with a red cross. The name George was made fashionable by the royal family. The future Queen Anne married Prince George of Denmark in 1683 and there have been six kings of Great Britain with the name, starting with George I (1660–1727). He became king of Great Britain and Ireland on the death of Queen Anne in 1714.

George was also the name of the first President of the United States, George Washington (1732–99). Other notable Georges have been the English painter George Romney (1734–1802) and Sir George Rooke, the English admiral (1650–1709) who with Sir Cloudesley Shovel captured Gibralter in 1704. Sir George Wolf (1821–1905) was the social reformer, lay preacher and founder in 1844 of the YMCA and finally another famous George was the Irish dramatist, George Bernard Shaw (1856–1950).

Geraint (b) Welsh from Greek roots; 'old'. A medieval name revived by the Victorians.

Gerald (b), **Geraldine** (g) Teutonic; 'ruler of the spear'. Diminutives are **Gerry, Gerrie**.

Gerard (b) A variant of Gerald and, like Gerald, popular in the Middle Ages and revived in the nineteenth century. Gerard is the hero of Reade's romance, set in the fifteenth century, *The Cloister and the Hearth*. The poet Gerard Manley Hopkins (1844–89), a Roman Catholic convert, wrote the famous *The Wreck of the Deutschland*.

Gideon (b) Hebrew; 'feller of men'; biblical.

Gilbert (b) Old German; 'bright pledge'. In vogue during the Middle Ages. St Gilbert of Sempringham (*c.* 1083–1189) founded an order of monks and nuns. He lived to be over 100 and was canonized by Pope Innocent III.

Giles (b) Probably Greek; 'young goat'. Athenian hermit saint (died *c.* 700), patron saint of beggars, lepers and cripples.

Gillian (g) English form of Julia. Variants include **Gill, Gilly, Jill**.

Glen, Glenn, Glynn (b) Gaelic; 'mountain valley, usually forming the course of a stream'. Popularized by the romances of Sir Walter Scott.

Glenda, Glennis, Glynis, Glynnis (g) Feminine variants of **Glen**. The British actress and politician Glenda Jackson (1937–) received an Academy award for her role in the 1970 film *Women in Love*, from the novel by D.H. Lawrence, and is also noted for her performance in *Sunday Bloody Sunday* and in the television series *Elizabeth R*.

Gloria (g) Latin; 'fame'. A modern first name.

Gordon (b) Scottish; 'from the three-cornered hill'. Sir

Gordon Richards (1904–1986) was one of the most successful flat-race jockeys ever. By 1952 he had established the world record of winning rides and in 1953, the year he won the Epsom Derby on Pinza, he received his knighthood. In 1954 he retired from racing to concentrate on training. Gordon Banks (1937–) is the famous footballer, whose astonishing skills in the 1966 World Cup final helped England beat West Germany during extra time.

Grace (g) Latin; 'thanks'. One of the abstract 'virtue' names favoured by the Puritans in the seventeenth century. In Roman mythology the Three Graces were the daughters of Zeus, goddesses who distributed joy and who were friends and companions of the Muses. Girls recently named Grace may have been named after the 1950s screen star Grace Kelly, though the name has long been fashionable in Ireland, where it has been used for the legendary heroine, Grania.

Graham, Grahame (b) Probably Celtic; 'from the grey house', though origin uncertain.

Grant (b) Old French; 'big, great'. From the surname.

Greg, Gregory (b) Greek; 'watchman, watchful'. A name used by the early Christians. Sixteen popes have been called Gregory, perhaps the most noteworthy of whom, Gregory XIII (1502–1585), endowed many Roman colleges and also introduced the Gregorian calendar in 1582.

The actor Gregory Peck's first screen appearance brought him instant success and he went on to star in many notable films including, *To Kill a Mockingbird* (1963), for which he won an Academy Award for his role as the defence lawyer.

Greta (g) Norse, originally a contraction of Margaret. The Swedish film actress of the 1920s and 1930s, Greta Garbo, will be well remembered for her roles in such films as *Grand Hotel*, *Anna Karenina* and *Camille*.

Gretchen (g) A contraction of Margaret.

Guy (b) Possibly Old German; 'leader'. The Normans introduced the name to Britain and it became fairly common. Guy of Warwick, for example, is the name of the hero of a popular early fourteenth-century verse romance. The name fell into disfavour after the attempt by Guy Fawkes and other conspirators on 5th November 1605 to blow up the king, his ministers and both the Houses of Parliament and to re-establish the Roman Catholic religion. Discovered in a vault under the Houses of Parliament with thirty-six barrels of gunpowder at the ready, Fawkes was tried, sentenced and hanged. The failure of the plot is celebrated on 5th November every year with bonfires and firework displays. The name returned to favour again in the 19th century.

Gwen, Gwenda, Gwendaline, Gwendolen, Gwendoline, Gwendolyn (g) Celtic; 'white browed, fair'. Gwendolen Harleth is the name of the heroine of George Eliot's last novel, *Daniel Deronda*, published in 1876. The artist Gwen John (1876–1939), a Catholic convert, settled and worked in France, spending much of her time with the Dominican nuns at Meudon. She was the sister of the painter, Augustus John, and became the close friend of the sculptor Rodin and the philosopher Maritain.

Gwyn (b), **Gwynne, Gwyneth** (g) Celtic; 'white'.

60

Hans (b) Variant of John.

Hamish (b) Scottish variant of James.

Hannah (g) Hebrew; early version of Anne. During the earlier part of her life the writer, Hannah More (1745–1833), moved in the best literary circles and wrote verses and dramas, including the tragedy *Percy*, produced by Garrick in 1777. Later she concentrated on trying to improve the conditions of poor people. Her tract *The Shepherd of Salisbury Plain* is amongst her most popular works.

Harold, Harald (b) Norse; 'great general, great commander'. Introduced to Britain by the Danes and was the name of two kings of England. Harold I (died 1040) called 'Harefoot', was the son of Canute, and the second one was Harold II, who reigned for only ten months in 1066 and who was defeated and killed at the Battle of Hastings. Harold Abrahams, the British athlete, who won the 100 metres gold medal in the 1924 Olympics, will be familiar to cinema-goers. His story formed the basis of the popular film *Chariots of Fire*. Diminutives of the name include **Hal** and **Harry**.

Harriet (g) Teutonic; 'home-rule'. Female form of the diminutive Harry.

Harrison (b) From the surname.

Harry (b) Though often given as a name in its own right is also a contraction of Henry and occasionally a diminutive of Harold.

Hartley (b) Old English; 'deer meadow'.

Harvey (b) Celtic; 'bitter', derived from the Breton Harvé or Hervé meaning warrior. Harvey Smith is the well known equestrian.

Hayley (g) Possibly taken from a surname.

Hazel (g) Teutonic; from the name of the small nut-bearing tree.

Heather (g) from the Scottish name, now in general use, for the flowering shrub, Erica. The name was especially popular at the turn of the nineteenth century.

Hebe (g) Name of the Greek goddess of youth, who had the powers of rejuvenation. Since Hebe was also cup-bearer to the gods the word has also been used to mean a waitress.

Hector (b) Greek; 'defender, anchor'. In Greek mythology the Trojan hero, son of Priam and Hecuba, who killed Patroclus and was himself slain by Achilles. Hector Berlioz (1803–69), the French composer, played a major role in the development of Romantic music. Originally a medical student, he turned to music against his father's wishes, eventually entering the Paris Conservatoire in 1826. His works include the *Symphonie Fantastique*, which expresses his feelings for the actress who became his wife, Harriet Smithson; the symphony *Harold in Italy*, based on a poem by Byron and written for Paganini; the *Grande Messe des Morts* and the opera *Les Troyens* (the Trojans), which was never performed in its entirety during his lifetime.

Heidi (g) German diminutive of Adelaide, popularized by the children's story.

Helen, Helena, Helene (g) Greek; 'light'. In Greek mythology Helen was the beautiful wife of Menelaus, king of Sparta. She was seduced by Paris who took her to Troy and this precipitated the Trojan War. St Helena was the mother of the Emperor Constantine who, according to some legends, was British, the daughter of an innkeeper. It is said that she discovered the True Cross and that she founded the basilica at Bethlehem. In literature Helena is the heroine of Shakespeare's *All's Well that Ends Well* and one of the central characters in *A Midsummer Night's Dream*. Helen of Kirkconnell, according to an old ballad, dies when she throws herself in front of her lover, to save him from being shot by a rival. Helen was also the name of the heroine of *The Tenant of Wildfell Hall* (published 1848) by Anne Brontë. The name has many variants including **Aileen, Eileen, Elaine, Eleanor, Ellen, Ellic**.

Henrietta (g) Feminine form of Henry. Henrietta Maria (1609–69) was the French wife of Charles I of England whose Roman Catholic beliefs made her unpopular with the people. *Henrietta Temple* is the title of a novel by Disraeli, published in 1837.

Henry (b) Old German; 'home-rule'. This was a name much favoured by European royalty and aristocracy through the ages. In England eight kings have been called Henry.

Henry Holland (1746-1806), the architect, designed the original Brighton Pavilion. Henry Rowe Schoolcraft (1793-1864), the American ethnologist, commanded an expedition which discovered the sources of the Mississippi. Sir Henry Irving (1838-1919) was the leading English actor of his day, and the first to receive a knighthood. Henry James (1843-1916), the novelist, author of over one hundred short stories, playwright and travel writer was born in New York. He later spent many years in England and was naturalized a British citizen in 1915.

Herbert (b) Teutonic; 'bright army'. A name introduced by the Normans, it is both a first name and also one of the oldest surnames in England.

Herman (b) Old German; 'army man'. The American writer Herman Melville (1819-91) used his experiences on board a whaler in his story *Moby Dick* (1851).

Hermia, Hermione (g) Greek; Feminine form of Hermes, who was, in Greek mythology, the messenger of the gods and inventor of the lyre. Hermia is a character in Shakespeare's *A Midsummer Night's Dream*, Hermonie appears in *The Winter's Tale*. Modern Hermiones include the comedienne, Hermione Gingold.

Hew (b) Welsh variant of Hugh.

Hilary, Hillary, Hilaire (b) and (g) 'cheerful'. Hilary Term in the English law courts and at Oxford is named in honour of St Hilary (*c*. 300-368), Bishop of Poitiers. Another saint,

Hilary of Arles (*c.* 403–49), became Bishop of Arles. The writer (Joseph) Hilaire Belloc (1870–1953) is best known for his nonsensical verse for children including, *The Bad Child's Book of Beasts*, and for his travel books.

Hilda (g) Teutonic; 'battle maid'. St Hilda (614–80) founded the monastery at Whitby in Yorkshire, England. The name has long been popular in northern England.

Hiram (b) Hebrew; 'noble brother'.

Holly, Hollie (g) From the plant name.

Honor (g) Latin; 'honour'.

Hope (g) One of the abstract virtue names. It was much used by the Puritans.

Horace, Horatio (b), **Horatia** (g) Latin; 'time, hour, punctual'. Popular with the ancient Romans and revived during the Renaissance. Horatio Viscount Nelson (1758–1805), the British Admiral, helped further to popularize the name.

Hortensia, Hortense (g) Latin; 'gardener'.

Howard (b) Origin and meaning uncertain but originally a surname.

Howell, Hywel (b) Celtic; 'eminent'.

Hugh, Hugo, Hubert (b) Teutonic; 'bright of mind, bright spirit'. The name was popularized by several saints including St Hugh of Lincoln, a 13th-century child-saint, whose story formed the basis for various legends and themes in literature. St Hubert (656–727), whose saint's day is 3rd November, was said to be a hunter converted to Catholicism by the apparition of a crucifix between the horns of the stag he was about to kill.

Hugh Gaitskell (1906–63) became an MP in 1945. He was elected Leader of the Labour Party in 1955 and held the position until his death.

Humphrey, Humfrey (b) Teutonic; 'giant peace'. The name has been in use since the Middle Ages. Humphrey Repton (1752–1818), the English landscape gardener (a term which he coined), designed around 200 parks and gardens as well as writing various books on gardening. Humphrey Bogart (1899–1957) the American tough-guy screen antihero, known for his lisp and his trenchcoat, will be remembered for his portrayal of the private eye, Sam Spade, in *The Maltese Falcon*. He was also acclaimed for his role in the classic *Casablanca* in which he played Rick.

Hyacinth (g) Greek; 'purple'. Mythological.

Ian, Iain (b) Scottish forms of John.

Imogen, Imogine (g) Anglo-Saxon; 'daughter' or perhaps 'last born', or Latin; 'image'.

India (g) from the name of the country.

Ingram (b) Teutonic; 'Ing's raven'. Ing was a legendary Scandinavian hero. Also a surname.

Ingrid (g) Norwegian; 'Ing's ride'.

Iona, Ione (g) Celtic; from the island in the Hebrides.

Irene (g) Greek; 'messenger of peace'.

Iris, Irys (g) Greek; 'rainbow'.

Irma (g) Teutonic; 'maid of high degree'.

Isaac (b) Hebrew; biblical; 'laughter'. Sometimes spelt **Izaac** or **Izaak**. The son of Abraham and Sarah in the Bible. A name used in Britain after the Reformation move away from saints' names. Isaac Merritt was an American manufacturer of sewing machines.

Isabel, Isobel, Isabelle, Isabella (g) Variants of Elizabeth, more common in Scotland, France, Italy and Spain but in use in Britain since the fourteenth century. In Shakespeare's comedy *Measure for Measure* Isabella is the sister of Claudio. Keats' poem *Isabella or the Pot of Basil* published in 1820 is based on the *Decameron* by Boccaccio.

Isadora (g) Greek; 'gift of Isis'. The masculine form Isidor is much less common. Isadora Duncan (1878–1927) developed a new style of dancing, based on Greek classical art.

Isolde, Isolde, Isolda, Iseult, Iseut, Isolt, Yseult, Ysolt (g) Celtic; 'spectacle' or perhaps 'fair damsel'. In Arthurian legend she was the daughter of the Duke of Brittany who loves Tristram. The name was revived by Wagner's music drama *Tristan und Isolde*.

Ivan (b) Russian form of John.

Ivo (b) Celtic form of John, from the Breton Yves.

Ivor (b) Possibly Teutonic; 'clinging' or from the Welsh 'lord'. The Welsh actor, dramatist and composer Ivor Novello (1893–1951) wrote the popular World War I song, *Keep the home fires burning*. He was also the author, composer and leading man of four successive 'Ruritanian' musical plays staged at Drury Lane during the 1930s.

Jackson (b) English; 'son of Jack'. The US artist Jackson Pollock developed the painting method known as 'action painting'.

Jacob, Jake (b) Hebrew; biblical; 'the supplanter'. The son of Isaac and Rebecca and twin of Esau in the bible. Always popular within the Jewish community, the name attained general favour at the time of the Reformation. *Jacon Faithful*, the novel by Marryat, published in 1834, tells the story of a river lighterman. Sir Jacob Epstein (1880–1959), was born in New York but lived in England from 1905, becoming a British subject. His commissions, which have often caused controversy, include *Night and Day* for the London Transport building, *Rima*, in Hyde Park, London, and the marble *Genesis*.

Jacqueline (g) French feminine form of Jacques. A diminutive is **Jackie**.

Jamal (b) Arabic; 'handsome'.

James (b) English form of the Hebrew, Jacob; biblical. The name of three early Christian saints: the apostle St James 'the Great', son of the fisherman Zebedee, who was beheaded in AD 44; St James 'the Just', eldest among the 'brethren' of Jesus and the apostle St James 'the Younger'. The name also has very strong royal associations, particularly in Scotland where there have been seven kings with the name — the last two also being kings of England. Famous people with the name include James Thomson (1700–48), the Scottish poet; the founder of the English canal system, James Brindley (1716–1722); James Cook (1728–79) the navigator; James Watt (1736–1819) the Scottish civil engineer; the Labour Premier James Ramsay MacDonald (1866–1937) and the Irish novelist James Joyce (1882–1941). Diminutives and variants include **Jamie, Jim, Jimmy, Jaimie, Jan, Jimmie, Seamus**. A feminine version **Jamesina** also exists.

Jane, Jayne (g) Feminine forms of John, probably via the Old French Jehane. Jane Austen (1775–1817) was one of the greatest English novelists. The American leading lady Jayne Mansfield (born Vera Jane Palmer) (1932–67) helped to make fashionable the spelling 'Jayne'. Diminutives: **Janey, Janie**.

Janet, Jannet, Janette, Janice, Janine (g) Originally diminutives of Jane, these are now popular as independent names, as are the many compounds of Jane, such as Mary Jane, Jennifer Jane, Amanda Jane and Sarah Jane.

Jared (b) A modern name.

Jasmin, Jasmine (g) From the flower, originally a Persian name.

Jason (b) Greek; 'a healer'. One of the principal characters in Greek legend, he undertook the expedition to recover the Golden Fleece. Jason Robards Jnr, the American actor, son of stage actor Jason Robards, is best-known for his performance in the 1961 film version of F. Scott-Fitzgerald's *Tender is the Night*.

Jasper (b) Persian; 'master of the treasure'. Variants include **Jaspar, Caspar, Gaspar, Gaspard** and **Kaspar**.

Jean, Jeanna, Jeanne, Jeanie, Jeannette (g) Variants of Jane and Joan. Jean is the Scottish form, derived from the French, Jehane.

Jefferson (b) from the surname. It gained popularity in the USA in honour of the third President, Thomas Jefferson.

Jeff, Jeffrey (b) Alternative spelling of Geoffrey.

Jem (b) and (g), **Jemima, Jemma, Mima** (g) Arabic; 'a dove' or Hebrew; 'handsome as the day'.

Jennifer, Jenifer, Jenefer, Jenni, Jennie, Jenny, Jen (g) Jennifer is an English form of the Celtic 'Guinevere', meaning 'white wave'. Its popularity outside Cornwall stems only from the twentieth century. Jenny (and its variants) is both a name given independently and a diminutive of Jennifer and of Jane. The soprano, known as the Swedish nightingale, Jenny Lind (1820–87), was one of the most popular and highest-paid concert artists. She used the greatest part of her earnings to found and endow musical scholarships and charities in England and Sweden.

Jeremiah (b) Hebrew; 'appointed by God'.

Jeremy (b) From Jeremiah and more frequently used in Britain. The English philosopher, Jeremy Bentham (1748–1832), was the man who promoted Utilitarianism. He was also a founder of University College, London, where his skeleton, dressed in his clothes, is preserved.

Jermaine (b) Possibly from a surname meaning 'closely akin, brother, sister, cousin', 'genuine, true' or 'German'.

Jermyn (b) Teutonic; 'bright'.

Jerome, Jerram, Jeronim (b) Greek; 'holy name'. St Jerome (Eusebius Sophronius Hieronymus) (*c.* 342–420), was a great writer and scholar.

Jesse (b) Hebrew; biblical; 'the true God, God exists'. In Christian art the genealogy of Christ, according to St Matthew's gospel, is often depicted as a tree which springs from Jesse, the father of David, which bears the ancestors of Christ as its fruit. The Tree of Jesse, as it is known, is based on the prophecy of Isaiah that: 'there shall come forth a rod out of the stem of Jesse, and a branch shall grow out of his roots', and is frequently found in churches dating from the Middle Ages particularly as a stained-glass window.

Sir Jesse Boot (1850–1931), the Nottinghamshire drug manufacturer, started the chain of chemist's shops which still bear his name and which, by the time of his death, numbered over a thousand branches. Jesse Owens, the American athlete, was the star of the 1936 Olympics in Berlin, winning no less than four gold medals.

Jessica (g) Hebrew; 'God is looking'. The diminutive Jessie is also sometimes given independently. *Jessica's First Prayer*, published in the 1860s, was a best-selling religious story.

Jethro (b) Hebrew; 'abundance'.

Jill, Jilly (g) Contractions of Gillian.

Joachim (b) Hebrew; biblical; 'appointed of the Lord'. The name of a twelfth-century Italian mystic, Joachim of Floris.

Joan, Joanna, Joanne, Jo-Anne (g) Variants of Johanna, Hebrew; 'grace of the Lord'. The Australian soprano, Joan Sutherland (1926–   ), is world famous for her beautiful singing.

Jocelin, Jocelyn (b) and (g), **Joceline, Jocelyne, Jocelind, Jocelynd, Joslyn** (g) Origin obscure. Perhaps derived from the Breton St Josse. Introduced by the Normans and originally a masculine name only. Jocelin de Brakelond, a Benedictine monk living at the end of the twelfth century in Bury St Edmunds, wrote a chronicle of his abbey from 1173–1202 which inspired Carlyle's *Past and Present*. The name has been used for girls since the end of the nineteenth century.

Jock (b) Scottish diminutive for John.

Jody, Jodi (b) and (g), **Jodie** (g) Modern names, probably derived from Judy. Popularized by the actress Jodie Foster.

Joel (b) Hebrew; biblical; 'Jehovah is God'. Sometimes given to girls, with variants: **Joelle, Joela, Joella**.

John (b) Hebrew; 'God has favoured' or 'God is merciful'. John is used in its various forms throughout Europe, the Middle East and in former colonies and territories of European countries.

73

A consistently fashionable boy's name for five centuries, its popularity is mainly due to St John the Evangelist and St John the Baptist — although some eighty other saints bear the name as well as twenty-one popes and two antipopes. Only one king of England has been called John (1199–1216) and he was unpopular; but the name has strong royal and aristocratic connections throughout Europe as well as literary and legendary associations. These include Little John, one of the companions of Robin Hood; John Bull, a character who represents England in Arbuthnot's pamphlets, and John Gilpin, the central character in Cowper's poem about an eventful horse ride. In the last few years the name has lost some popularity as a first name, although it still remains a favourite second name.

Jonah, Jonas (b) Hebrew; 'dove', but it used to mean 'to bring ill luck to'.

Jonathan (b) Hebrew; 'the Lord's gift', 'the Lord has given'. Biblical name which rose to popularity after the Reformation. It is sometimes used as a variant of John; its diminutive is Jon. Jonathan Swift (1667–1745) was educated at Trinity College, Dublin, where he was censured for disciplinary offences. He is best known for *Gulliver's Travels*, published in 1726.

Jordan (b) and (g) Hebrew; 'descender'.

Jonquil (g) From the flower.

Joseph (b) Hebrew; biblical; 'God shall multiply, God shall add'. The favourite son of Jacob in the Bible, whose jealous brothers took him to Egypt and sold him to Potiphar. In the New Testament, he was a carpenter of Nazareth and the husband of the Virgin Mary. Joseph of Arimathea, buried the body of Jesus in his own tomb.

74

Joseph Andrews published in 1742, was the first novel by Henry Fielding, written as a skit on Richardson's *Pamela*, whose brother Joseph Andrews is supposed to be.

Josephine, Josephina (g) Feminine form of Joseph. Perhaps the most notable Josephine was the wife of Napoleon Bonaparte. Diminutives include **Jo** and **Josie**.

Josh, Joshua (b) Hebrew; biblical; 'Jehovah is salvation'. The American mariner Joshua Slocum undertook in 1895 a three-year solo voyage around the world on the sloop *Spray*.

Josiah (b) Hebrew; 'Jehovah supports'. The eighteenth-century English potter, Josiah Wedgwood, patented a beautiful cream-coloured earthenware of Neo-classical design; Queen's Ware, in honour of the factory's patroness, Queen Charlotte. He used the most modern methods in his factory and sponsored a canal system to transport his wares from the factory to the ports of Liverpool and Bristol.

Joy (g) the virtue, used as a name. Favoured by the Puritans.

Joyce (g) Celtic; origin uncertain but probably from the Breton St Josse. Originally more commonly a boy's name. Returned to fashion at the turn of the nineteenth century.

Jude (b) Hebrew; 'praise the Lord'. St Jude, apostle and martyr, is the reputed author of the last Epistle in the New Testament.

Judith, Judy (g) Hebrew; biblical; 'a jewess'. **Judy**, a diminutive, is also found as an independent name. It owes much of its appeal to Judy Garland (1922–1969) (real name Frances Gumm) who charmed cinema audiences when she

75

played Dorothy in the 1939 film *The Wizard of Oz*. Judy is also the name of Punch's wife in the puppet show drama, *Punch and Judy*. Other forms and diminutives include **Judie**, **Jude** and **Jodie**. In the Bible, Judith, whose story is told in the book of the Apocrypha, is said to have ventured into the tent of Holofernes, the enemy general of Nebuchadnezzar, cut off his head and so saved the town of Bethulia. The story has inspired many writers and artists throughout the centuries.

Julia, Julie (g) Latin; feminine forms of Julius. Julia was the name of many women of the ancient Roman Julian *gens*, including the sister and the daughter of Gaius Julius Caesar; the daughter of the Emperor Augustus and also the wife of the Emperor Septimus Severus and mother of Caracalla. *Julia* was the title of a 1977 film, based on Lillian Hellman's memoir of a friendship between two women. The film starred Jane Fonda as Lillian Hellman, and Vanessa Redgrave as her friend Julia, whose political activities brought her into conflict with the Nazis.

Julian (b) Latin; a derivative of the Greek name Julius, which means 'first growth of beard, downy beard'. Associated with Julius Caesar.

Juliana (g) Feminine version of Julius, and also the source of the names Gillian and Jill.

Juliet, Juliette, Julie (g) Originally pet forms of Julia, now used independently. Juliet owes its popularity to the heroine of Shakespeare's play *Romeo and Juliet*. Julie is the name of the heroine of Rousseau's *La Nouvelle Heloise* (1761).

76

Julius (b) See Julian.

June (g) Name derived from the month.

Justin (b), **Justine, Justina** (g) Latin; 'just'. St Justin was a first-century Christian martyr.

Kane (b) Gaelic; 'tribute'.

Karen, Karin, Karina (g) Danish; 'pure'.

Katherine, Kate, Katy, Kathleen (g) See Catherine.

Kay, Kaye (g) Originally a diminutive of Karen, Katherine and other names beginning with K.

Keith (b) Gaelic; 'wind' or Celtic; 'wood'. From the surname.

Kelly, Kelli, Kellie (g) From the Irish surname.

Kelvin (b) Probably from the surname.

Kenneth (b) Celtic or Gaelic; 'handsome'. Scottish royal name. Kenneth I, known as Macalpine, king of the Dalriada Scots, who conquered the Picts. Kenneth Grahame

78

(1859–1922) wrote *The Wind in the Willows*.

Kent (b) Celtic; 'chief', or possibly 'white'. St Kentigern, the apostle of Cumbria, was a first-century missionary.

Kerry, Kerri, Kerrie, Kerie, Keri (g) From the Irish place-name.

Kevin (b) Irish version of Kenneth.

Keziah (g) Hebrew; biblical, one of the three beautiful daughters of Job.

Kiely, Keely, Keeley, Keelie (g) Modern name, probably derived from an Irish surname.

Kieron, Kieren, Kiaran, Kiraren, Kyran, Ciaren, Ciaran, Kier (b) Celtic; 'swarthy', 'dark one'.

Kim (b) and (g) Anglo-Saxon; 'chief'.

Kimberley (g) From the surname or named after the diamond mine, Kimberley in South Africa.

Kirk (b) Scottish; 'church'.

Kirsten, Kirstie, Kirsty, Kirstin (g) Contractions of Christine or Christian.

Kyle (b) and (g) Gaelic; 'channel, strait'.

Kylie, Kiley, Kaylee, Kayleigh (g) Aboriginal, 'boomerang', 'throwing stick'.

Lana (g) Latin; 'woolly' or Greek; 'light'. Popularized by Lana Turner (real name Julia Turner), the Hollywood star of the 1940s.

Lance, Lancelot, Launcelot (b) Latin; 'boy-servant'.

Lara (g) Eastern European form of Laura.

Laura, Lauren, Laurel, Lori (g) from the Latin; 'laurel, bay tree'. The name Laura was immortalized by the Italian poet Petrarch (1304–74), who wrote a long series of love poems in praise of Laura, whose identity is unknown. The paintings of Dama Laura Knight (1877–1980) portrayed the life of gipsies and circus people. Lauren was popularized by the beautiful American actress Lauren Bacall (real name Betty Jean Perske), who made her first screen appearance opposite Humphrey Bogart, later to be her husband.

Laurence, Lawrence (b) Greek; 'laurel, bay tree' or Latin;

'of Laurentum'. Brought into favour by several saints of which the best known is the third-century saint. He was born in Spain but was brought to Rome where he became Deacon, in charge of the Church treasures. In the persecution of Valerian, he was executed by the cruel death of slowly roasting on a gridiron. The name first began to gain popularity in Britain after the Norman conquest. Notable modern-day people with the name include the explorer Lawrence Oates (1880–1912). He was the member of Scott's Antarctic Expedition who walked out to certain death in a blizzard, certain that his lameness caused by frostbite would hinder the chances of his companions to get back safely. Lawrence Durrell, the poet and novelist, spent much of his life in the Eastern Mediterranean, where much of his writing is set. His *Alexandria Quartet* was completed in 1960. Sir Laurence Olivier, the celebrated actor and producer, has played an enormous variety of roles, from the great Shakespearian characters to Archie Rice in Osborne's *The Entertainer*. Variants of the name include **Laurie, Lawrie, Larry, Lonnie, Lorry** and **Lorne**.

Lavinia (g) Latin; 'a woman from Lavinium'. A fashionable Renaissance name, also in favour during the eighteenth century, with its taste for all things classical.

Leanne, Lianne (g) Modern name, perhaps based on Leigh Ann.

Leigh, Lee (b) and (g) Anglo-Saxon; 'meadow'. The form Leigh is more common for girls, with Lee usually reserved for boys.

Lena (g) Pet form of names like Leonora, Helena, Eleanora, Magdalena and now also an independent name.

81

Lennox (b) Gaelic; 'chieftain'.

Leo, Leon (b), **Leona, Leonie** (g) from the Greek; 'lion'. Leo is the constellation lying between Cancer and Virgo and also the fifth sign of the zodiac, named after the constellation. There is also a constellation called Leo Minor, lying between the Great Bear and Leo. There were thirteen popes called Leo, the first of which was the first century St Leo, called 'the Great', whilst Leo X was the celebrated art patron, Giovanni de' Medici, the second son of Lorenzo the Magnificent.

Leonard (b) Teutonic; 'lion-strong'. Leonardo da Vinci (1452–1519) the Florentine painter, sculptor, architect and engineer was one of the greatest Renaissance figures. Quite apart from his genius as an artist he had a wide knowledge of most of the sciences — he almost discovered the circulation of the blood; he also studied aeronautics and he invented the earliest armoured fighting vehicle.

Leroy (b) French; 'king'.

Leslie (b), **Lesley** (g) Gaelic; possibly 'low lying meadow'. From the Scottish surname/place name and used as a first name only from the nineteenth century.

Lewis (b) Celtic; possibly 'lion like' or French; 'famous', from Louis. In *The History of John Bull* by Arbuthnot, the French king Louis XIV is called Lewis Baboon. Lewis Carroll was the pseudonym of Charles Lutwidge Dodgson (1832–98), who wrote *Alice's Adventures in Wonderland* and *Through the Looking-glass* both illustrated by Tenniel.

Liam (b) Irish version of William.

Lianne (g) See Leanne.

Lilian, Liliane, Lily, Lilly, Lilias, Lilli, Lilyan (g) Probably from the Latin; 'lily', but may also be pet forms of Elizabeth.

Linda, Lynda (g) Originally a contraction of names like Belinda, Rosalinda, Melinda, but used as a name in its own right since the turn of the nineteenth century. **Lindy** is also used.

Lindsey, Lindsay, Linsay, Linsey, Lyndsay, Lyndsey (g) (and sometimes [b]) Possibly Teutonic; 'of gentle speech' or an Old English place name, indicating the presence of linden or lime trees. Later a Scottish surname. Originally a boy's name only, but now mainly reserved for girls.

Lionel (b) Greek; 'little lion'.

Lisa, Lise, Liza (g) diminutives of Elizabeth.

Llewellyn, Llywellyn, Llew (b) Celtic; 'lion-like'.

Lloyd (b) Celtic; 'grey'.

Lois (g) Originally a contraction of Aloisia; 'famous war'.

Lola (g) diminutive of the Spanish Dolores, meaning 'grief'.

Lorna (g), **Lorne** (b) and (g) Anglo-Saxon; 'love lorn, lost'. *Lorna Doone*, the novel by R. D. Blackmore, published in 1869, introduced the name of Lorna, its heroine, who it transpires, is from a Scottish noble family, stolen from her parents by the wicked Doones.

Louis (b) Derived from the Old German or French,

83

meaning 'famous' or 'famous fighter'. See **Lewis**. Among notable people with the name was the French sculptor, Louis Roubillac (also spelt Roubiliac), who in 1738 made his home in London and carved the statue of Handel for Vauxhall Gardens which assured his popularity. The French general, Louis Montcalm (1712–59), was mortally wounded during the battle with Wolfe on the Heights of Abraham, Quebec. Wolfe himself also died at the moment of his victory. Lord Louis Mountbatten was viceroy and governor general of India, presiding over the transfer of power. In 1955 he was made first sea lord. The Belfast-born poet, Louis MacNeice (1907–63), wrote several successful verse plays for radio. (Daniel) Louis Armstrong (1900–71), better known as 'Satchmo', was an American jazz trumpeter, singer and show-business personality.

Louise, Louisa (g) Feminine versions of Louis. Louisa is the name of the heroine of Sheridan's comic opera *The Duenna*, produced in 1775. Louisa May Alcott (1832–88) was the American author of children's stories, among them the enormously successful classic *Little Women*. In the twentieth century Louise may have been popularized by the song made famous by the French singer, Maurice Chevalier.

Lucian, Lucien, Lucius (b), **Lucy, Lucie, Lucia** (g) Latin; 'born in daylight'. Lucius, a mythical king of Britain, was supposed to have been the first Christian convert. Lucian was a first century Greek writer and satirist, author of *Dialogues of the Gods*. St Lucy, whose feast day is 13th December, is the patron saint of the blind. The male forms of the name are rare nowadays, except for people like the British artist Lucian Freud, grandson of Sigmund. The female forms are still popular. Variants of the feminine form include: **Luce, Lucilla, Lucinda, Lucetta, Lucille, Lucienne**.

84

Luke, Luc (b) Greek; 'coming from Luciana'. St Luke the Evangelist was the constant companion of St Paul, whose life he recorded. He is called the 'beloved physician' and there is also a legend that he was an artist and painted portraits of the Virgin Mary and Jesus. He is the patron saint of doctors and of painters. The name Luke, used infrequently in Britain since the Middle Ages, has recently become very popular.

Luther (b) A variant of Lothair, Lothario, meaning 'famous', 'of renown'. Its use may have been encouraged by the German religious reformer, Martin Luther (1483–1546) who was also a gifted musician. A modern-day person with the name, Martin Luther King (the black American civil rights leader), received an honorary doctorate from Yale in 1964, the Nobel peace prize and also the Kennedy peace prize. He was assassinated in 1968.

Lydia (g) Greek; 'woman of Lydia'. (Lydia was a district in Asia Minor whose people were believed to have been the first to coin money as well as being famed for their music.)

Lyn, Lynn (b) or (g), **Lynne, Lynette, Linnet, Linnette** (g) Anglo-Saxon; 'brook' or 'waterfall, cascade'. Lynette may come from linnet, the song-bird. It was made popular by Tennyson's *Gareth and Lynette*, one of the *Idylls of the King* published in 1872.

Lynton (b) Anglo-Saxon; 'town by a waterfall'.

Mabel (g) Contraction of Amabel, 'lovable', Mabel was a favourite nineteenth-century name. In Ireland the name became **Maeve**, after one of the Irish legendary heroines. Mabel Lucie Attwell (1879–1964) is known for her writing for and illustrations of children.

Madeline, Madeleine, Magdalen, Magdalene, Magdelena, Maddy, Madge, Magda (g) Derived from the Hebrew; 'woman of Magdala'. St Mary Magdalene, the penitent sinner, was a favourite subject of Renaissance art. She has given her name (pronounced in this case 'Maudlen') to one of the colleges of both Oxford and Cambridge. The word 'maudlin' meaning weeping, tearful, is an allusion to paintings of her, as she is often shown crying. Her feast day is 22nd July.

Magnus (b) Latin; 'great'. Saint's name and Scandinavian royal name.

Maire (g) Irish form of Mary.

Malachi (b) Hebrew; biblical; 'God's messenger'. Old Testament name, favoured after the Reformation. St Malachy (*c.* 1094–1148) introduced the Cistercian order to Ireland.

Malcolm (b) Celtic; 'servant of Columba'. The name of four Scottish kings including Malcolm III called Canmore ('Great Head'), who was the son of King Duncan, murdered by Macbeth.

Mamie (g) Originally a diminutive of Margaret, now used independently.

Mandy (g) (and variants) See Amanda.

Manfred (b) Old German; 'man of peace'. Introduced by the Normans. *Manfred* is the name of a dramatic poem by Byron.

Manuel (b) See Emanuel.

Marc (b) See Mark.

Marcella, Marcelle, Marcelia, Marcellina (g) Variants of the female form of Marcellus, which is, in its turn, a diminutive of **Marcus, Mars,** the god of war.

Marcia, Marcie (g) Female forms of Marcus.

Marcus (b) Latin; connected with Mars, the god of war. He was also a god of agriculture and protector of cattle.

Margaret (g) Greek; 'a pearl', which incorporates the Persian 'child of light', because the Persians believed that pearls were made either by raindrops falling into the oyster and being changed into pearls by moonbeams or else by the pearl oyster rising to the surface of the water at night to worship the moon, the pearls being formed by the congealing of the dew by moonlight.

St Margaret (*c.* 1045–93) of Scotland, born in Hungary and wife of King Malcolm Canmore (see Malcolm) was apparently beautiful, pious and cultured. There have been many other royal Margarets in Britain – these include Margaret Tudor and Princess Margaret, sister of Queen Elizabeth II – and others throughout Europe. Dame Margaret Rutherford (1892–1972) the English actress, made her debut in a pantomime at the Old Vic in 1925 and first appeared on the screen in 1936. Gradually she began to be recognized as a comedienne and her notable roles included Miss Prism in *The Importance of Being Earnest*, Madame Arcati in *Blithe Spirit* and Mrs Malaprop in *The Rivals*. There are countless variants and diminutives of Margaret including: **Maggie, Margo, Margot, Mamie, Margareta, Marge, Margie, Megan, Meghan, Molly, Peg, Peggy**. Also linked is **Marguerite**, meaning 'daisy', from the French. Its diminutives include **Rita**.

Maria, Marian, Marion, Mariana, Marianne, Marie (g) See Mary.

Marigold (g) One of the flower names, from 'Mary gold', probably referring to the Virgin Mary.

Marilyn (g) See Mary.

Marina (g) Latin; 'of the sea'. Literary; Pericles' daughter in

Shakespeare's play by that name and Jacopo Foscari's wife in Byron's historical tragedy, *The Two Foscari* (published in 1821). Princess Marina of Greece and Denmark (1906–68), wife of George, Duke of Kent, brought the name to the attention of the British.

Marius (b) Latin; 'of Mars'.

Marjorie, Margory, Marjery (g) Scottish variants of Margaret. Known from the nursery rhyme.

Mark, Marc (b) Probably derived from the Roman god, Mars. (See Marcus.) St Mark the Evangelist is traditionally the author of one of the gospels. He was a travelling companion of St Paul and Barnabas on their first missionary journey and he is later said to have spent twelve years in Libya and to have preached and later been martyred in Alexandria. His body was then taken to Venice where he is now the patron of the city. He is represented in art accompanied by a winged lion, and sometimes with a pen and the book of his gospel. His feast day is the 25th April, when, according to superstition, everyone fated to be married or to die, pass, in procession, the porch of the church. The swimming champion Mark Spitz won a record total of seven gold medals in the 1972 Olympic Games in Munich.

The name Mark was popular throughout the Middle Ages and returned to popularity in the 19th century. The variant **Marc** is now gaining favour.

Marsha (g) Latin; 'of Mars'.

Martha (g) Aramaic; biblical; 'a lady'. St Martha is represented in the Bible as someone devoted to running the home. She is the patron of housewives and has given the name an association with humility. She is usually depicted in art with a bunch of keys attached to her girdle and carrying a ladle. The name has seen a recent revival.

Martin (b), **Martina** (g) French form of the Latin Martius, 'belonging to Mars'. Popularized by several early saints, particularly St Martin of Tours (*c.* 316–*c.* 400) born in Hungary, who is said to have cut his cloak in two and given half to a ragged beggar. He is reputed to have worked many miracles. The patron saint of tavern keepers, he is commemorated on 11th November. Five popes have also been called Martin. In literature, Martin is the hero of Charles Dickens' novel, *Martin Chuzzlewit*, who is in love with the orphan Mary Graham.

Marvin, Marven, Marvyn, Mervin, Mervyn (b) Probably from a surname. Anglo-Saxon; 'famous friend'. May have been popularized in recent years by the actor Lee Marvin, the soul singer Marvin Gaye and the boxer Marvin Hagler.

Mary (g) The English form of the Hebrew Miriam, meaning 'bitterness'. A name with many variants and the most popular girls' name of all throughout Europe, except in the post-Reformation period. Its popularity is due to the Virgin Mary, mother of Christ, with whom other names, such as Madonna, Dolores and Annunciata are also associated. Incidents in the life of the Virgin are described in the New Testament books of Matthew, Luke, John and the Acts. She is the subject of many legends and only Christ has been as often portrayed in Renaissance art.

The name has strong Royal associations as well, including Mary I of England (1516–58) the daughter of Henry VIII and Catharine of Aragon. Mary Queen of Scots (1542–87) was a beautiful, accomplished, but tragic figure, finally beheaded on a charge of conspiring against the life of the English queen,

Elizabeth I. Her life is the subject of a tragedy by Schiller and appears in the works of many other authors. Mary Shelley (1797–1851), the second wife of the poet, Percy Bysshe Shelley, wrote *Frankenstein or the Modern Prometheus*. Maria Montessori (1870–1952), the Italian educationalist, developed the educational method for young children which bears her name. The American actress, Mary Pickford, first appeared on stage when only five years old. Her films included *Poor Little Rich Girl*. Variants of Mary include: **Maria, Marie, Maureen, Marilyn, Marylyn, Mari, Marian, Marion, Marianne, Mariana, Mariel, Marika, May, Moira, Molly, Maura, Mair, Mairi, Mariam, Marisa, Mariska, Marisella**.

Matthew, Mathias (b) Hebrew; biblical; 'gift of the Lord'. Popularized by St Matthew the Apostle and Evangelist, who was a tax collector in the service of the Romans before he became one of Christ's disciples. Little is known about his life, though legend says he died in Ethiopia.

Maureen (g) Irish contraction of Mary. Maureen Connolly, 'Little Mo', (1934–69) was one of the world's great tennis players. In 1953 she was the first woman to win the USA, the French, the English and the Australian singles titles.

Maurice, Morris (b) Latin; 'a moor'.

Mavis (g) Old name for a song thrush but only in use in modern times and probably the invention of the English popular novelist, Marie Corelli (1855–1924).

Max, Maxi (b) and (g), **Maximilian, Maxim** (b), **Maxie, Maxime, Maxine** (b) Latin; 'greatest, biggest'. Formerly a name favoured by Middle European royalty and chosen in

Britain and the USA by parents of German extraction in particular. Its use is becoming more widespread. An English variant, **Maxwell**, is also found. Notable people with the name Max include Max Schreck (1879–1936), the German actor; the Austrian theatrical producer Max Reinhardt (1873–1943) who directed the 1935 classic *A Midsummer Night's Dream* and Maximilian Schell, the Austrian leading man whose films include *Judgment at Nuremberg* and *The Odessa File*.

May (g) Name of the month and also a pet form of Mary and of Margaret.

Maynard (b) Old German; 'firmness, strength'. John Maynard Keynes (1883–1946), the economist, set forward the theory of full employment.

Melanie (g) Greek; 'dark-complexioned, black'. Saint's name. Popularized in the twentieth century by the book and film, *Gone with the Wind*.

Melinda, Melina (g) Origin obscure, possibly Greek; 'of the ash tree' or 'song'.

Melissa, Melise (g) Greek; 'bee, honey'. Used by sixteenth-century Italian poets, including Ariosto in *Orlando Furioso*, and used in England from the eighteenth century.

Melody (g) Old English abstract name.

Melvin, Melvyn (b) Celtic; 'chief'. The American Melvin Sheppard won the 1908 Olympic 800 and 1500 metres at White City, London, and also helped the USA achieve victory in the medley relay.

Mercedes (g) Spanish; from Maria de las Mercedes, Mary of the Mercies.

Meredith (b) and (g) Welsh; 'sea protector' or 'greatness'.

Mercy (g) Latin; 'pity'.

Mervin, Mervyn, Marvyn (b) Anglo-Saxon; 'famous friend'.

Michael, Michel, Mitchell (b), **Michaela, Michelle, Michele, Micheline** (g) Hebrew; 'like to God'. Michael is one of the most popular names for boys in England, in common use since the twelfth century. Its appeal comes from the Archangel Michael, highly revered since the Middle Ages and a favourite subject of Renaissance artists.

Michael Faraday (1791–1867), the son of a blacksmith, was a distinguished chemist and natural philosopher and made many important discoveries in physics and electricity.

The name Michelle was given a boost by the Beatles' song, which was a track on their long playing record *Rubber Soul* released for Christmas 1965.

Diminutives of Michael include **Mick, Mickey, Mike** and **Mitch** whilst diminutives of the feminine variants include **Mickie, Mich** and **Michou**.

Mildred (g) Old English; 'mild power'. The diminutives are **Milly** or **Millie**.

Miles, Myles (b) Origin obscure. Perhaps Slavonic; 'merciful', Greek; 'millstone' or Old German; 'loved, beloved'. The American jazz trumpeter Miles Davis (1926–   ) is a well-known musician with the name.

Milton (b) Old English; 'settlement, village near a mill'. Place name and surname. Made famous by John Milton (1608–74) the great English poet, born at Bread Street, Cheapside, London and educated at St Paul's School and Christchurch, Cambridge. Author of *Lycidas*, *Paradise Lost*, *Paradise Regained* and *Samson Agonistes*.

Mina, Minna, Minella, Minnie (g) Teutonic; 'love'.

Mirabel, Mirabelle, Mirabella (g) Latin; 'wonderful'. Now a girl's name, but a masculine form of the name, **Mirabell**, is used by Fletcher for the hero of his comedy, acted in 1621, *The Wild-Goose Chase*. It was also used in Congreve's comedy *The Way of the World*, produced in 1700, Mirabell is the lover of Millamant, niece of Lady Wishfort.

Miranda (g) Latin; 'worthy of admiration'. The daughter of Prospero in Shakespeare's *The Tempest*.

Miriam (g) Hebrew, and oldest, form of Mary.

Moira, Moyra, Maura (g) Celtic; 'soft'.

Mona, Monica, Monique (g) Possibly Greek; 'unique'.

Morag (g) Gaelic; 'sun'.

Morgan (b) and occasionally (g) Welsh; 'sea-dweller'.

Morris, Maurice (b) See Maurice.

Mortimer (b) Celtic; 'sea warrior'.

Moses (b) Either Coptic; 'saved from the water' or Hebrew;

94

'law giver'; biblical. The stockbroker philanthropist, Sir Moses Haim Montefiore (1784–1885), was an indefatigable worker for Jewish rights.

Mungo (b) Celtic; 'lovable'. Mungo Park (1771–1806) the Scottish explorer and surgeon told the story of his incredible journeys in Africa in *Travels in the Interior of Africa* (1799).

Muriel, Meriel, Meryl (g) Celtic; 'sea white'. *Muriel* was a 1962 film by the French director Alain Resnais. The successful actress Meryl Streep (1949–   ) made her first screen appearance in *Julia* in 1977. In 1979 she won an Academy Award for her role in *Kramer vs. Kramer.*

Murray (b) Celtic; 'a seaman'. Scottish clan name.

Myrna (g) Arabic; 'myrrh'. The thirties star, Myrna Loy, (born Myrna Williams) may have helped promote the name.

Myron (b) Name of the celebrated ancient Greek sculptor who worked mainly in bronze, and who is known for his Discobolus and Marsyas.

Nadia, Nadine (g) Russian; 'hope'. Chuck Berry's catchy song *Nadine* was a hit record in 1964.

Nancy (g) Originally a variant of Anne, Hannah or Agnes, but it is now used independently. The variant **Nanette** also occurs.

Naomi (g) Hebrew; 'fine one, pleasant one'; biblical. A favourite choice of the Puritans.

Natalie, Nathalie, Natasha, Natalia (g) From the Latin; 'birth', suggesting the birth of Christ, and therefore particularly suitable for girls born on Christmas Day.

Nathan (b) Hebrew; 'gift'.

Nathaniel (b) Hebrew; 'gift of God'; biblical.

Neal, Neil, Neill, Nial (b) Celtic; 'champion'.

Nell, Nellie, Nelly (g) Originally pet forms of Helen and Eleanor, although also used independently. Nell Gwynne was the mistress of Charles II of England. 'Little Nell', Nell Trent, was the heroine of Dickens' *The Old Curiosity Shop*. Nellie Melba (1861–1931), the Australian prima donna, took her professional name from her birthplace, Melbourne.

Nelson (b) Popularized by the great sailor.

Nerys (g) Welsh; 'lord'.

Neville (b) French; 'new town'. Originally a surname, it was introduced by the Normans.

Nicholas, Nicolas, Nicol (b), **Nicole, Nicola, Nicolette, Nicky, Nikki** (g) Nicholas is from the Greek; 'victory of the people'. The fourth-century St Nicholas of Myra (or Bari), the patron saint of Russia, youth, sailors, merchants, thieves and pawnbrokers, is believed by many to have been a purely legendary figure. Because his feast day, 6th December, falls at Christmas time his story has become interwoven with the Christmas story.

Nigel (b) **Nigella** (g) Latin; 'black'.

Nina (g) A diminutive of Anne, also used independently.

Noel, Nowell (b), **Noelle, Nola, Noeline** (g) French; 'Christmas'. Another name for children born on Christmas Day.

Norman (b) Germanic or Old English; 'northman'. Until recently it was used mainly in Scotland.

97

Octavia (g) Latin; 'eighth child'. In Roman history, the sister of the emperor Augustus. Her first husband was Claudius Marcellus, and after his death she married Mark Antony, who left her for Cleopatra. Another Octavia was the daughter of the emperor Claudius by Messalina. She married Nero who divorced her and then had her put to death.

Odelia, Odette, Odile (g) Teutonic; 'of the fatherland'.

Olaf (b) Old Norse; 'ancestor's relics'. The name of five kings of Norway of which the first was the saint who helped diffuse Christianity throughout his kingdom. Several churches in Britain are dedicated to him, including that in Tooley Street, Southwark, London. Tooley is itself a corruption of the saint's name.

Olga (g) Old Norse; 'holy'.

Olive, Olivia, Olivette (g) From the Mediterranean tree. The name has existed in Britain since the Middle Ages. The form Olivia has been popularized by its literary associations. Olivia is one of the main characters in Shakespeare's *Twelfth Night*. An Olivia also appears in Wycherley's comedy *The Plain Dealer*, produced in 1677 and is the name of one of Dr Primrose's daughters in *The Vicar of Wakefield* by Oliver Goldsmith.

Oliver (b) Possibly Old French; 'olive'. The name was brought to Britain by the Normans and popularized by the Charlemagne cycle of legends, in which he is the companion in arms of Roland. The name later fell out of favour because of its associations with the Lord Protector Oliver Cromwell who ruled from 1653–8, though it was once more in use in the eighteenth century. Oliver Goldsmith (1728–1774), the poet and prose writer, is probably the most famous eighteenth-century figure with the name. His best-known prose work is *The Vicar of Wakefield* and he was also the author of the comedy *She Stoops to Conquer*. The name Oliver enjoyed a return to favour in the nineteenth century, with the taste for the medieval. Its revival was helped by Charles Dickens' novel *Oliver Twist* published in 1837–8.

Olwen (g) Celtic; 'white track'.

Omar (b) Arabic; 'most high'.

Ophelia (g) Greek; meaning uncertain, possibly 'serpent', 'help' or 'wisdom'. Ophelia was the daughter of Polonius in Shakespeare's *Hamlet*, who becomes mad and drowns. The subject was a favourite one for Pre-Raphaelite artists, perhaps the best-known representation being that painted by Millais in 1851–52.

Orlando (b) Italian; 'fame of the land'. Orlando Gibbons (1583–1625), the English organist and virginalist, wrote church music and madrigals, including *Dainty Fine Sweet Bird* and *The Silver Swan*.

Orson (b) Italian; 'a bear'. Orson Welles, the versatile actor, writer, director and producer, numbers amongst his many films *Citizen Kane* and *The Third Man*.

Oscar (b) Old English; 'divine spear'.

Ottilie (g) Old German; 'fatherland'.

Owen (b) Origin uncertain but may be a Welsh form of Eugenius, 'well born'. Variants include **Owain, Ywain, Ewen** and **Eugene**. Owen Glendower or Glyndwr (*c*. 1350–1416) was a Welsh chief who claimed to be a descendant of Llewellyn, the last Prince of Wales. He led the Welsh rebellion against the English king Henry IV. Owen Glendower is a prominent figure in Shakespeare's play, *Henry IV*.

Orville (b) French; 'gold town'.

Pamela (g) Greek; 'all sweetness'. A name invented by Sir Philip Sidney for one of the beautiful daughters of the king in his prose romance *Arcadia*, which he started to write in 1580 for the amusement of his sister. The name became popular when Samuel Richardson used it for the heroine of *Pamela, or Virtue Rewarded*, published in 1740.

Pascale (g) Hebrew; 'of the Passover'; Latin, 'of Easter'.

Patience (g) One of the abstract virtues.

Patricia (g) Latin; 'patrician'. Feminine form of Patrick. Diminutives include **Pat, Patty, Patsy, Trish, Tricia, Trisha, Trixie, Patrice**.

Patrick (b) Latin; 'patrician'. St Patrick, the patron saint of Ireland, whose festival is on 17th March, was born late in the fourth century in Wales, France or Scotland. He was seized by pirates and taken to Ireland. He later escaped to

France and some time afterwards returned, via Britain, to Ireland where he founded a mission settlement. Variants and diminutives of the name Patrick include **Pat**, **Paddy**, **Patrice**, **Padraig**, **Padrig**.

Paul (b), **Paula**, **Pauline**, **Paulina**, **Paulette** (g) Greek; 'small'. Popularized by several saints, in particular St Paul the Apostle, the first-century follower of Jesus, whose history is known from the Acts of the Apostles and the Epistles of St Paul in the New Testament. Famous people with the name have included the English watercolour painter, Paul Sandby (1725–1809), an original member of the Royal Academy. Among his favourite subjects were views of Windsor and Eton and the scenery of Wales. The French physicist, Paul Langevin (1872–1946), is best known for his theory of magnetism and for the study he made of the molecular structure of gases. The writer Paul Scott (1920–1978) won the prestigious Booker Prize for Fiction in 1977 for his novel about India, *Staying On*. His *The Raj Quartet* became an enormously successful television series entitled *The Jewel in the Crown*. The black American singer and actor, Paul Robeson (1898–1976) appeared in a number of films including *Showboat*.

Penelope (g) Greek; possibly 'weaver'. In Greek mythology she was the wife of Odysseus. During his absence she was courted by many suitors but put them off by saying she had to finish weaving a robe for her father-in-law, and by undoing each night the weaving she had completed during the day. She represents the faithful wife. The pet form of the name, Penny, occurs independently.

Perdita (g) Latin; 'lost'. The name was probably invented by William Shakespeare for the princess, abandoned as a baby on the shore of Bohemia and raised by a shepherd in the play, *The Winter's Tale.* The actress Mary Robinson (1758–1800) was known as 'Perdita' as she played this part.

Perry (b) Derived from Peregrine, Latin; 'wanderer'.

Peter (b) **Peta, Petra, Petronia, Petronella, Petrina** (g) Greek, from the Aramaic; 'rock' or 'stone'. Derives its widespread use mainly from the leader of the twelve apostles. Originally a fisherman of Galilee, his missionary work took him throughout Asia Minor. Tradition has it that he worked for twenty-five years in Rome. In most paintings he is shown holding the keys to heaven. The name Peter, which was first used in Britain in the form Piers, has been one of the favourite names for boys for many centuries. The female forms have never enjoyed the same favour.

Philip, Phillip, Philippe (b), **Philippa, Pippa** (g) Greek; 'fond of horses, lover of horses'. The use of both the masculine and feminine forms of the name were encouraged by St Philip, the apostle, who appears infrequently in the gospels though he is associated with the Feeding of the Five Thousand. Many legends surround his later life. The name has many royal associations including Philip II of Macedonia, father of Alexander the Great.

The use of the female form, Philippa, was encouraged by the marriage, in 1328, in York, of Edward III with Philippa of Hainault.

Piers (b) An early contraction of Peter, from the French.

Polly (g) Originally a diminutive of Mary but now used independently. The name occurs in several nursery rhymes and songs such as: *Polly put the kettle on, Little Polly Perkins, Little Polly Flinders* and *Miss Polly had a dolly.* Polly Peachum is one of the main characters in John Gay's *The Beggar's Opera*, produced in 1729 and its sequel, *Polly*, published the following year, though its stage production was prohibited by the lord chamberlain.

Pollyanna (g) Hebrew; 'bitter' and 'graceful'. A name made familiar by the cheery heroine of Eleanor H. Porter's novels.

Poppy (g) From the flower.

Portia (g) Latin; 'hog'. The name was made popular by the heroine of Shakespeare's *The Merchant of Venice*.

Primrose (g) From the flower.

Priscilla (g) Latin; 'of olden times'. Favoured by the Puritans. Priscilla was the heroine of *The Courtship of Miles Standish* by Longfellow. Diminutives include **Prissy** and **Cilla**, popularized in recent years as a name in its own right, by TV personality, Cilla Black, born Priscilla White.

Prudence (g) Latin; 'prudent'. Well-loved by the Puritans.

Prunella (g) Old French; 'plum-coloured'. Its pet forms include **Pru**, **Prue** and **Prudie**.

Psyche (g) Greek; 'the spirit, the human soul'.

Quentin, Quintin (b), **Quintella, Quintina** (g) Latin; 'the fifth child'.

Quiller (b) Teutonic; 'fledgling'.

Rab (b) Scottish pet form of Robert.

Rachel, Rachael, Rachele, Rachelle, Raquel (g) Hebrew; 'ewe'; biblical. The wife of Jacob in the Bible. Variants and diminutives of the name include **Rae, Ray, Raye, Rayette, Rochelle, Shelley, Shelly**.

Ralph, Ralf, Rafe (b) From the Old English Radulf or Rannulf meaning 'wolf counsel'. Ralph Flambard succeeded Lanfranc as chief adviser to William II. He held the office of Justiciar. He became Bishop of Durham in 1099 but ministered to the vices of the king. Imprisoned by Henry II he escaped to France where he became Bishop of Lisieux.

Ramsay (b) Teutonic; 'the strong'. James Ramsay MacDonald (1866–1937) educated at a Scottish Board School, became, in 1924, the first Labour prime minister.

Randal, Randle (b) Form of Randolph.

Randolf, Ranolf (b) Old English; 'house wolf' or 'shield wolf'. A name which survived the Norman conquest. The pet form, Randy, is sometimes used and is popular in the USA. An alternative spelling is **Randolph**.

Raymond, Raymund (b) Old French; 'wise protection'. In recent times notable people with the name have included the French President, Raymond Poincaré (1860–1934); the American doyen of detective novels, Raymond Chandler (1888–1959) and the footballer Ray Clements.

Rebecca, Rebekah (g) Hebrew; 'a snare'. Biblica, the wife of Isaac. In fashion from the Reformation but probably owes its more recent use to the children's novel by Kate Douglas Wiggin, *Rebecca of Sunnybrook Farm* (1903). The story was filmed three times. The 1917 version starred Mary Pickford. In 1932 Marian Nixon played Rebecca and in 1938, Shirley Temple took the title role. The diminutive of Rebecca is **Becky**.

Reginald (b) Teutonic; 'judgment power'.

Renée, Renata (g) French/Latin; 'reborn'.

Rex (b) Latin; 'king'.

Reuben (b) Hebrew; 'behold a son'; biblical. In use in Britain by the Puritans and always popular as a Jewish name.

Rhett (b) Probably from Rhys, its use comes from the film,

Gone with the Wind (1939), in which the dashing Rhett Butler was played by Clark Gable.

Rhoda (g) Greek; 'from Rhodes'.

Rhona (g) Old Welsh; 'fair'.

Rhys (b) Welsh; 'impetuous'. Pronounced and sometimes spelt Reece.

Richard (b) Old English or German; 'stern ruler'. Introduced by the Normans. The name of three remarkable English monarchs, Richard has been in vogue since the Middle Ages. Famous people through the ages with the name have included the chronicler Richard of Cirencester (1335–1401); Richard of Wallingford (1292–1335), abbot of St Albans and known as the father of English trigonometry; Richard Neville, Earl of Warwick (1428–71) 'the King-maker', the most powerful adherent of the Yorkist faction in the Wars of the Roses. They also include the dandy, Richard 'Beau' Nash (1674–1762), who transformed Bath into a fashionable resort; Sir Richard Arkwright (1732–1792), originally a hairdresser, the inventor of the 'spinning frame' for cotton mills; Richard Cobden (1804–65), the economist; Richard Wagner (1813–83) the German composer who revolutionized the music of his time and Richard Burton (1925–84), the Welsh stage and screen actor.

There are numerous diminutives of the name, including **Diccon, Dick, Dickie, Dicky, Ritch, Ritchie, Rick**.

Robert (b) Old German; 'bright fame'. Popular since the Norman conquest, Robert was the name of the father of William the Conqueror. He was known, apparently with good reason, as Robert le Diable (Robert the Devil). Robert

107

de Bruis, a Norman knight who came to England with William the Conqueror was the ancestor of the illustrious Scottish Bruce family, several of whom were called Robert. The best known is the hero of the Scottish War of Independence. Rob Roy (Red Robert) Macgregor (1671–1734) was the subject of many stories of daring deeds and cunning escapes and of generous gifts to the poor. His history forms the basis of the novel *Rob Roy* by Sir Walter Scott, published in 1817. Sir Robert Peel (1788–1850) organized the formation of the police force and twice became Prime Minister. Robert Southey (1774–1843) was born at Bristol, the son of a linen-draper. One of the Lake Poets, he was made Poet Laureate in 1813. Another leading poet was Robert Bridges (1844–1930).

Pet forms of Robert include **Rob**, **Robbie**, **Rab**, **Rabbie**, **Bob**, **Bobbie**, **Bobby**, **Robin**.

Roberta (g) Feminine form of the above.

Robin, Robyn (b), **Robynne** (g) Originally a diminutive of Robert, the name is now usually given independently, though its use as a girl's name is modern. The name is also associated with the bird. The name Robin is found widely in English legend and literature. The legends of Robin Hood have always been particular favourites and the mischievous sprite Robin Goodfellow appears in, for example, Shakespeare's *A Midsummer Night's Dream*.

Rodney (b) from the surname. Old English; perhaps 'road servant'. Diminutives: **Roddy**, **Roddie**.

Roderick (b), **Roderica** (g) Old German; 'famous ruler'. Roderick Douglas, the light middleweight boxer, was born in 1964 in Bow, London, of West Indian parents.

Roger (b) Teutonic; 'spear of fame'. Introduced to England by the Normans, and soon a favourite name.

Roland, Rowland (b) Teutonic; perhaps 'spear of fame' or 'famed throughout the land'. Roland was the most famous of Charlemagne's paladins and the subject of various legends, in particular the early-12th-century *Song of Roland* and, as Orlando, in Ariosto's *Orlando Furioso*. More recently, Sir Rowland Hill (1795–1879) was the inventor of the penny postage system, introduced in 1840. Variants include: **Orlando, Rollo** and **Rolando** and the name also exists in a feminine form, **Rolande**.

Ronald (b) Scottish contraction of Reginald, 'great warrior', used as a name in its own right.

Rose, Rosa, Rosabel, Rosabelle, Rosalie, Rosina, Rosita, Rosanna, Roseanne, Rosalba, Rosaline, Rosalind, Rosamond, Rosamund, Rosy, Rozanne, Roslyn, Roslynne, Rosebud (g) All variants of the Teutonic *hros*, 'a horse' though the name has been used for many centuries in the Latin, floral sense. Rosalba, from the Latin, means 'white rose'. Rosalind, from Latin and Spanish, 'pretty as a rose' — its popularity comes from the heroine in Shakespeare's *As You Like It*. Rosamond was popularized by the legend, based on fact, of Rosamond Clifford, mistress of Henry II, who kept her in a house as impenetrable as a maze. Queen Eleanor, however, found the way in, and poisoned her in about 1176.

Rosemary, Rosemarie (g) From the name of the plant, also a compound of the name **Rose**.

Ross (b) From the surname. Perhaps Teutonic; 'a horse' or Gaelic; 'one who lives at the promontory'.

Rowan (b), **Rowena** (g) Celtic; 'white skirt'.

Roxanne, Roxana (g) Persian; 'dawn'. Roxana was the Persian wife of Alexander the Great. In Defoe's *Roxana or the Fortunate Mistress*, the eponymous heroine receives her name by accident, because of a dance she performs.

Roy (b) Celtic; 'red' or French; 'king'.

Rupert (b) Teutonic; 'bright fame'. A form of Robert. Made popular by Prince Rupert (1619–82), the 'Mad Cavalier'. The poet Rupert Brooke (1887–1915) caught in his work the patriotic spirit of the early part of the Great War and the later disillusionment.

Russell (b) Old French; 'red-head'. Originally a surname. Pet forms include **Russ, Rusty**.

Ruth (g) Hebrew; biblical; origin obscure but possibly 'vision of beauty' or 'friend'. An Old Testament name, favoured by the Puritans.

Ryan (b) Irish; from a surname, possibly 'red'.

Sacha (b) Greek; 'helper of mankind'. From the same root, through the Russian, as Alexander.

Saffron (g) Arabic; 'crocus'.

Sally (g) A diminutive of Sarah, used as a name in its own right.

Samuel (b) Hebrew; 'name of God'; biblical. A popular name from the time of the Reformation. Famous bearers of the name include Samuel Richardson (1689–1761), the novelist; Samuel Johnson (1709–84) the lexicographer, poet and critic; Samuel Morse (1791–1872), American inventor of the magnetic telegraph and the Morse code and Samuel Palmer (1805–81), the watercolour painter. Other prominent people include: Samuel Smiles (1812–1904), author of *Self-Help*; Samuel Ryder (1859–1936) the nursery and seedsman, donor of the professional golfing cup which bears his name and Sam Wanamaker, the American actor and director.

Sandra, Sandie (g), **Sandy, Sandro** (b) and (g) Diminutives of Alexandra and Alexander, also given independently.

Sarah, Sara, Sally, Zara (g) Hebrew; 'princess'; biblical. Abraham's wife in the Bible. Sarah has been used in Britain since the twelfth century. Sarah Siddons, the English tragic actress, was the eldest of twelve children of the actor manager of a small travelling theatre company, and made her name as Isabella in Southerne's *The Fatal Marriage*. Her most celebrated role was Lady Macbeth. One play she appeared in was Congreve's *The Mourning Bride*, where she took the part of Zara, the Moorish queen. Zara is a variant of the name Sarah. In recent years it has received attention as the name of the daughter of Princess Anne. Pet forms of Sarah include **Sadie, Sady** and **Sal**.

Saul (b) Hebrew; 'the asked for'; biblical.

Scarlett (g) After the red colour. It was made popular by Margaret Mitchell's novel of the American South during the Civil War *Gone with the Wind* which became an Academy Award-winning film. Vivien Leigh was voted best actress for her role as Scarlett O'Hara, the beautiful, yet spoilt, heroine.

Scott (b) From the surname, meaning a Scotsman. A diminutive is **Scottie**.

Sean, Shaun, Shawn, Shane (b) Sean, pronounced Shawn, is the Irish form of John. Shane was popularized by the 1953 western of that name, starring Alan Ladd.

Selina, Sillina, Celina, Celine, Selena, Selene (g) Greek; 'moon', mythological or from the French, Celine, originally from the Latin; 'heaven'.

Selwyn (b) Old English; 'house friend'.

Serena (g) Latin; 'calm, serene'.

Seth (b) Hebrew; 'compensation'.

Seamus, Seumus (b) Irish forms of James.

Shane (b) See Sean.

Shannon (b) From the name of the river.

Sharlene (g) A modern name.

Sharon (g) Hebrew; 'flat area of land, plain'. From a place name.

Sheena (g) Irish form of Jane.

Sheila, Sheelagh, Shelagh (g) Irish form of Celia or Celicia.

Shelley, Shelly (g) Modern name, probably originally a pet form of Sheila or Sarah, or of names like Rachel, Michelle and Rochelle.

Sheri (g) from the French Cherie 'darling'.

Sheyla, Shayla (g) Probably variants of Sheila.

Shirley (g) and occasionally (b) Old English; 'sheer lea'. Originally a place name and then a surname, it was later used as a boy's first name. In 1849 a novel by Charlotte Brontë was published in which the heroine, Shirley Keeldar, (based on the author's sister, Emily) has been given a boy's name because her parents had wanted a son. Shirley then began to be used as a girl's name. Later the feminine use increased when the Vicar of Shirley named a new strain of poppy he had cultivated, Shirley, and the name then became a flower name. Finally the name rose to great popularity as a girl's name when babies born in the 1930s were called after the American child-star, Shirley Temple.

Sibyl, Sibylla, Sibille, Sibel (g) Greek; 'a prophetess'.

Sidney (b) Originally a surname, probably a contraction of the French St Denis, which, in its turn, comes from Dionysius. The name of the versatile Elizabethan, Sir Philip Sidney. Sidney Greenstreet was a major Hollywood star in the 1940s. His films include *The Maltese Falcon*, *Casablanca* and *The Woman in White*.

Sidonia, Sidonie, Sidony (g) Latin; 'fine cloth', possibly with reference to the shroud in which Jesus' body was wrapped.

Simon (b), **Simone** (g) Greek; 'snub-nosed'.

Siobhan (g) Irish feminine form of Sean.

Sonia, Sonya (g) Slavonic; 'wise'.

Sophia, Sophie, Sophy (g) Greek; 'wisdom'. The name of the church (now a mosque) in Istanbul, which was built by the emperor Justinian, is Hagia Sophia (Divine Wisdom). Sophia was a favourite name in England in the eighteenth century and was the name of the heroine of Henry Fielding's *Tom Jones*, published in 1749, in which Sophia, the daughter of the neighbouring Squire Western, truly does live up to the meaning of her name.

Spencer (b) Old English; 'steward'. The British statesman, Spencer Perceval (1762–1812) was the only Prime Minister in Britain to have been murdered while in office. He was shot while entering the lobby of the House of Commons by a bankrupt, John Bellingham.

Stacey, Stacy (b) and (g) Contractions of Anastasia and Anastasius, meaning 'one who shall rise again'.

Stanley (b) Old English; 'stone-meadow'. Originally a place name and then a surname. As Prime Minister, Stanley Baldwin (1867–1947) faced many problems in Britain and overseas. His periods of office included the General Strike of 1926 and the abdication crisis of 1936–37. Sir Stanley Matthews (1915–   ) was the first footballer to receive a knighthood. During his long soccer career (from the age of 14 to 46 years of age) he played fifty-four games for England.

Stella (g) Latin; 'star'.

Stephen, Steven, Stefan (b), **Stephanie, Stephania, Stephana** (g) Greek; 'crown'. The feast day of St Stephen, who was the first Christian martyr, is 26th December. Ten popes took the name Stephen — one of them died two days after his election. The name was also a favourite with the royal houses of Europe during the Middle Ages. More modern Stephens include Stephen Collins Foster, the composer of *Camptown Races* and many other famous songs; the poet and critic Stephen Spender (1909–   ); and the American singer, Stevie Wonder.

Stewart, Stuart (b) A Scottish name, from the Anglo-Saxon; 'steward'. The pet form is usually **Stu**.

Stirling, Sterling (b) Old English; either 'excellent' or perhaps 'little star' (starling). The racing driver, Stirling Moss, won the British Grand Prix in 1955 and, with Tony Brooks, in 1957. Moss was the winner of the RAC's Campbell Memorial Trophy in 1957 and 1958. Amongst his other triumphs was the RAC's Hawthorne Memorial Trophy in 1961.

Susan, Susanna, Susannah, Suzanne, Suki (g) Hebrew; 'graceful white lily'; biblical. In the Bible, Susanna, the wife of Joakim, was surprised by two elders while taking a bath. Pet forms of the name include **Sue** and **Susie**.

Suzanne Lenglen (1899–1938), the French tennis star, was competing in the French hard court singles from the age of 15. She was unbeaten in thirty-two singles matches at Wimbledon and won the title every year from 1919 (the first time she had played on grass) to 1925, except for 1924 when her increasingly poor health forced her to retire. She was triple champion in France from 1919 to 1923 and in 1925 and 26. She turned professional in 1926.

Sylvia, Silvia (g) Latin; 'wood, forest'. Roman mythological name which was revived in the Renaissance and also favoured in the nineteenth century. *Sylvia's Lovers*, a novel by Mrs Gaskell published in 1863, tells the story of a farmer's daughter loved by a plain, honest man, while she in her turn is in love with a worthless sailor.

Tabitha (g) Aramaic; 'a gazelle'.

Tamara (g) Hebrew; 'palm tree'.

Tamsin (g) Contraction of Thomasina, a female form of Thomas. More popular in the West Country of England, particularly Cornwall. The pet forms **Tammy** and **Tammie** are also used independently.

Tanya, Tania, Tatiana (g) Tatiana was a third century martyr of the Orthodox church and the name was a Russian favourite. **Tanya** and **Tania** are pet forms of the name.

Tatum (g) Middle English; 'cheery'. Popularized recently by the precocious actress, Tatum O'Neil.

Terence, Terrance, Terry (b) Perhaps from the Latin; 'tender'. The Roman comic poet, Terence (c. 190–159 BC), was born at Carthage and brought to Rome as the slave of a Roman senator who educated him and whose name Terence he took when he was freed.

117

Teresa, Theresa, Terri, Terrie, Terry, Tess, Tessa, Teresita, Tracey, Tracy (g) Greek; 'reaper'. St Teresa (1515–82), the Spanish saint, canonized in 1622, was a mystic and a Carmelite reformer. A popular name, particularly with Roman Catholics.

Thea (g) Greek; 'goddess'.

Thelma (g) A literary name invented by Marie Corelli.

Theodora (g), **Theodore** (b) Greek; 'God's gift'.

Thomas (b) Aramaic; 'twin'; biblical. A very common name for boys since the Middle Ages. The name of a number of saints, including the Apostle, often called 'doubting Thomas' and St Thomas of Canterbury — Thomas à Becket (1118–70) — the Archbishop of Canterbury who was murdered in Canterbury Cathedral. It later became an extremely popular place of pilgrimage, as described by Chaucer in his *Canterbury Tales*. Thomas Gainsborough (1727–1788), was a famous and fashionable landscape and portrait artist. He was one of the founder members of the Royal Academy. Thomas Paine (1737–1809) the author of *The Rights of Man*, was the son of an ex-Quaker staymaker and Norfolk farmer. He was involved in the American War of Independence (he was the man who coined the phrase the United States of America) and, later, in the French Revolution.

Tiffany (g) Greek; 'manifestation, revelation of God'. Popularized by the 1961 film, *Breakfast at Tiffany's*, which starred Audrey Hepburn, George Peppard and Patricia Neal.

Tilda, Tilly (g) Contractions of Matilda, a Teutonic name meaning 'battle maid'. These names are now often given independently.

Timothy (b) Greek; 'honouring God' or perhaps 'honoured by God'.

Tina (g) Pet form of Christina, used independently.

Titus (b) Origin obscure, but perhaps Greek; 'I honour'. Titus Oates (1649–1705) had been discharged from various curacies and a naval chaplaincy for infamous conduct. He fabricated the Popish Plot, suggesting that there would be a massacre of Protestants by Roman Catholics and that the king would be assassinated. For his services in 'revealing' the plot he was rewarded, and became a hero. In 1685 he was convicted of perjury, pilloried, flogged and imprisoned. Later William III set him free and even gave him a pension.

Tobias, Toby (b) Hebrew; 'God is good'.

Tod, Todd (b) From the surname. Middle English; 'bundle, pack' or 'fox'.

Toya, Toyah, Toy (g) Meaning unknown. A modern-day pop singer and actress with the name is Toya Wilcox.

Tracey, Tracy (g) and (b) Probably originally a pet form of Theresa, and also a surname. Its popularity may in part be due to the actor Spencer Tracy (1900–1967), whose major films include *Captains Corageous*, for which he won an Oscar, and *Judgment at Nuremberg*.

Travis (b) Middle English; 'toll-gatherer'.

Trevor (b) Originally a Welsh surname meaning 'great village', the name is popular in England, Ireland and Wales, where the form **Trefor** is also found.

Trixie, Trixy (g) Latin; 'bringer of joy'.

Troy (b) Perhaps from the French place name, Troyes.

Trudie, Trudy (g) Old German; 'strength'.

Tudor (b) Welsh contraction of Theodore.

Tyrone (b) Possibly place name, from the Irish. Tyrone Power (1913–1958) appeared in numerous films in the 1930s, 1940s and 1950s and will be remembered for his portrayal of the masked hero of *The Mark of Zorro* (1940).

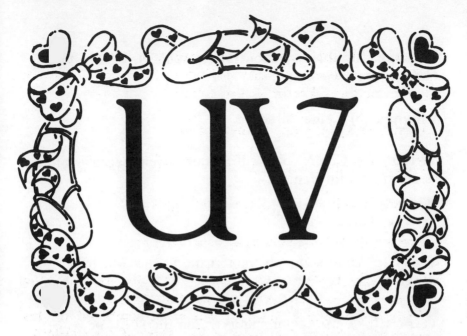

Una, Unity (b) Latin; 'one'. In Spenser's *Faerie Queen* Una represents the true religion. Una Stubbs, the actress and TV personality is a modern-day person with the name.

Ursula (g) Latin; 'female bear'. Saint's name.

Valentina (g), **Valentine** (b) and (g) Latin; 'strong'. St Valentine's Day has been steeped in custom since the fifteenth century. Tradition has it that it was the day on which the birds chose their mates. This custom has now developed into the practice of sending one's sweetheart a gift, or nowadays a greetings card.

Valerie (g) French feminine form of the above.

Vanessa (g) Invented by Jonathan Swift (1667–1745) as a pet name for Esther Vanhomrigh, using parts of her name.

The story of their relationship is told in Swift's poem, *Cadenus and Vanessa*.

Vaughan (b) Celtic; 'little'.

Venetia (g) Celtic; 'blessed'. Often given because of its associations with Venice.

Vera (g) Latin; 'true'.

Verity (g) One of the abstract virtue names which became popular with the Puritans.

Vernon (b) Latin; 'flourishing'. From the surname.

Veronica, Veronique (g) Latin; 'true image'. According to legend St Veronica took pity on Jesus as he made his way to be crucified and wiped the sweat from his brow with her handkerchief or veil. Miraculously the veil is said to have retained Christ's likeness. Popular in England only from the last century. The pet form is usually **Ronnie**.

Victor (b) Latin; 'victorious'. Saint's name. (Edwin John) Victor Pasmore, the artist, was one of the founders of the Euston Road group in the late 1930s.

Victoria (g) Latin; 'victorious'. Most modern Victorias are named after Queen Victoria (1819–1901) who became Queen on the death of her uncle, William IV, in 1837. Variants and pet forms of the name include **Vickie, Vicky, Vikki, Victoire, Victorine, Tory, Vita** (as in Vita Sackville-West, the novelist and poet), **Vitoria** and **Vicqui**.

Vincent (b) Latin; 'conquering'. Vincent Van Gogh (1853–90) was the famous Dutch painter whose best-known paintings include: *A Cornfield with Cypresses*, *The Yellow Chair* and *Sunflowers*. Pet forms include **Vin**, **Vince** and **Vinnie**.

Viola, Violet, Violette (g) Latin, English and French forms of the flower.

Vivian, Vivyan, Vyvyan (b), **Vivien, Vivienne** (g) Latin; 'alive'.

Wade (b) Teutonic; 'advancing'.

Waldo (b) Norse; 'power'.

Wallace (b) From the Scottish surname.

Wallis (g) From the surname, meaning Wales.

Walter (b) Old German; 'folk-ruler'. Introduced by the Normans. Famous people with the name have included Sir Walter Scott (1771–1832), the Scottish novelist and poet; Walter Sickert (1860–1942), the British Impressionist artist and Walter Huston (1884–1950) the American screen and stage actor, father of the director John Huston.

Wanda (g) Old German; 'stem, stock'.

Warren (b) Probably Teutonic; 'protecting friend', introduced by the Normans. Also common as a surname. Warren

Hastings (1732–1818) went out to India for the first time in 1750 as a writer in the service of the East India Company. In 1773 he was made governor general. On his return to England he was the subject of a parliamentary inquiry and was impeached at the bar of the House of Lords, for rapacity and oppression. After the trial, which lasted over seven years, he was acquitted but the case had ruined him financially. The actor Warren Beatty (1937–   ) has appeared in *Bonnie and Clyde*, *Shampoo* and *Reds*, amongst other films.

Washington (b) From the surname, derived from a place name.

Wayne (b) Teutonic; 'ancient waggon' or from Wainwright, 'wagon maker'. Originally a surname, now also used as a first name.

Wendy (g) Literary; used by Sir James Barrie in the play, *Peter Pan*.

Wesley (b) Anglo-Saxon; 'of the west meadow'. Sometimes given in honour of the eighteenth-century evangelists, John Wesley, the founder of Methodism and his brother Charles, the hymn writer.

Whitney (g) Old English; possibly 'elf battle'.

Wilfred, Wilfrid, Wilfried (b) Anglo-Saxon; 'resolute peace'. St Wilfrid (*c.* 634–709) is the patron saint of bakers. Wilfred Owen (1893–1918), the World War I poet, was killed in action on the Western Front just before the Armistice was signed. Wilfred Rhodes (1877–1973) started playing cricket for Yorkshire at the age of 21 and carried on playing first class cricket for some thirty-two years.

William (b) Teutonic; 'helmet of resolution'. Introduced into England in the eleventh century, it has been since then one of the most popular names for boys. The name has royal connections and has been the name of many notable men through the ages, including William Shakespeare (1564–1616). It is also the name of several saints. Diminutives include **Will, Willie, Willy, Bill, Billie, Billy, Willem** and the name is also found in the Welsh, French and Irish forms as **Gwilym, Gill, Gillot, Liam.**

Windsor (b) An English surname used as a first name.

Winston (b) Originally a place name from the Old English meaning either 'wines town' or 'conquering town', and then a surname. It was used as a first name in the Churchill family since the early seventeenth century. The popularity of the name stems from Sir Winston Churchill (1874–1965), the famous British statesman.

Winthrop (b) Teutonic; 'friendly village'.

Xanthe (g) Greek; 'yellow'.

Xavier (b), **Xaviera** (g) Arabic; 'splendid, bright'. A rare name, but sometimes used to commemorate St Francis Xavier (1506–52), the missionary, youngest son of the privy-councillor of the King of Navarre. See Francis.

Xenia (g) Greek; 'stranger'.

Yolanda, Yolande (g) Probably a form of Viola. Iolanthe is a variant of the name.

Yves (b), **Yvette, Yvonne, Yevette** (g) Variants of the Breton form of the Welsh name Evan, and thus of John.

Zachariah, Zackary, Zack, Zak, Zacky, Zaccheus, Zacchaeus, Zaccaria (b) Hebrew; 'God has remembered'.

Zara (g) See Sarah.

Zebedee (b) Hebrew; 'gift from the Lord'.

Zelda (g) Origin unknown, possibly from the Hebrew. The wife of the American novelist and short-story writer, F. Scott-Fitzgerald, was called Zelda.

Zena (g) pet form of Zenobia, the name of a Queen of Palmyra.

Zoe (g) Greek; 'life'. Its use in Britain is fairly recent, but it was the name of the third-century Christian martyr.